# THE GOLF SWING

## It's easier than you think

Chris Riddoch

The Golf Swing
http://www.TheGolfSwingZone.com

Image credits
Bigstock: cover, 45, 55, 61, 63, 67, 68, 69, 75, 113.
Florida Center for Instructional Technology: 107.
Fotosearch: 93.
Shutterstock: 3, 5, 13, 15, 33, 37, 77, 79, 101, 109.
Thinkstock: 1, 25, 105.

No copyright holder could be located for Bernard Darwin's book *Tee Shots and Others*.

*For Maya*

# Contents

# List of figures

# Acknowledgements

MANY FRIENDS AND COLLEAGUES have contributed both time and expertise to the creation of this book. Their insightful comments have been invaluable and I'm extremely grateful to all of them.

In particular, Dr Grant Trewartha (University of Bath) and Professor Colin Boreham (University College, Dublin) commented on scientific accuracy. Dr Sean Cumming (University of Bath) contributed valuable materials on coaching. Golfing colleagues Philip Lindner and Dick Moore advised on content, readability, and style. My wife Maya assisted with cover and interior design, and – most importantly – tolerated my hours at the computer with exceptional grace. Interactive Frontiers, Inc. (Plymouth, MI) kindly gave permission to use V1 swing analysis software in the design of the cover image.

I'm also hugely indebted to the many scientists around the world who carried out the high-quality research that makes the book possible. I apologise for being unable to cite all your work individually.

Chris Riddoch is a professor of sports science who has published more than 200 scientific articles on sport and exercise. A scratch golfer in his teens, he represented his college (Borough Road), his county (Cheshire), and had two trials for England (not selected, alas). He is married to Maya and they live in Stockholm.

# 1

# Introduction

THIS BOOK HAS JUST ONE AIM: to declutter our golfing brains. Because they're full. We try to understand how to swing a golf club, but the more we try, the deeper we descend into the swing theory quagmire. Unfortunately, we've transformed the golf swing from a natural, human striking skill – similar to a tennis serve, cricket shot, or baseball hit – into a complicated shopping list of things we don't understand and can't remember.

The internet has added further complexity, spawning a vast, electronic reservoir of diverging opinions about the golf swing, all easily accessible with just a few clicks of a mouse. Unfortunately, the golf swing has become a hugely complex creation, shrouded in mystery and confusion. The time must be ripe for a clearing-out exercise; we – the dazed and confused golfers – need a way out.

This book provides one. Using a scientific analysis of high-quality research, it cuts through the buzzing bewilderment by separating golf swing fact from golf swing fiction. The analysis uses only research published in scientific journals, ensuring that all source information has been subjected to a high level of scientific scrutiny. The book addresses two areas:

- ⚑ HOW HUMANS LEARN PHYSICAL SKILLS
- ⚑ HOW THE GOLF SWING WORKS.

It identifies five *key skills* – one mental and four physical – that are essential to making an effective golf swing. The book explains each skill in detail and outlines a simple, effective way to learn them. This approach combines the best scientific knowledge of not only golf swing mechanics, but also the powerful, innate biological systems that enable us to learn them. All golfers – from beginners to tour professionals – will benefit.

Part 1 explains the nature of the golf swing problem and how treating the swing as a long series of 'perfect' positions hinders learning. Part 2 describes how humans learn skills and explains the critical role of swing thoughts. Part 3 explains the golf swing's five key skills. Finally, Part 4 suggests a practical way forward – a way to make it happen.

In the interests of readability, individual scientific references haven't been included in the text; however, key concepts have been attributed as appropriate via endnotes. Annex 2 lists the scientific sources used to compile the book.

# Part 1
# The problem with the golf swing

*Solitary struggling with a recalcitrant club is essentially a good thing .... It is likely to become a deleterious process if it involves a reconsideration of all the theories proposed by all the pundits, followed by a trial of them all in turn. ... It is this conflict of ideas, the constant wondering if we might not do better some other way, which undermines the confidence and loses half crowns.*

—Bernard Darwin, 1911[1]

# 2

# Dazed and confused

**B**ERNARD DARWIN'S OBSERVATION suggests that information over-load has existed in golf for more than a century. And in the 100 years since, overload levels have increased inexorably, as we further develop technology to scrutinise the golf swing in ever-more forensic detail. Today, the amount of information about 'what moves where' during a golf swing is simply overwhelming. The volume of material disheartens us, its contradictions perplex us, and the jargon frustrates us. The big problem with today's golf swing is—it's too big a *problem*.

Unfortunately, humans don't have learning systems that can cope with large amounts of information. In fact, the human brain works in exactly the opposite way – to learn physical skills, it requires *simplicity*. But now, when we strive to improve our swings, where should we start? Should we swing on one plane or two? Should we stack or tilt? Or double shift? Is the thumbs-up swing better than the hammer or biokinetic swing? How do we supinate our left wrists? How do we know whether our power accumulators arc accumulating? Should we check our L factor, O factor, R factor, S factor, X factor, Triple X factor, Y factor, Z factor, crunch factor, mind factor, or smash factor?

Like a dissected animal, the golf swing's organs – together with innumerable systems for fitting them back together – fill the pages of magazines, books, and websites. And something new appears every week: an unremitting torrent of secrets, breakthroughs, discoveries, 'proven' new theories, and revolutionary methods— even 'magic' solutions. This state of confusion has prompted one swing coach to comment:

> *Today's golf swing is a mechanical jigsaw puzzle, in which one attempts to put together innumerable parts in a preconceived way …. There is always another piece of the puzzle to be found and worked on …. We are trapped in a web of mechanical complexity.*
>
> —Peter Lightbown, 2010[2]

## Professor Butt's self-operating napkin

Professor Butt raises a soupspoon to his mouth and spills some soup down his chin. Luckily, he has a system for cleaning it up. Tied to the soupspoon is a string that jerks a ladle, throwing a firecracker past a parrot. The parrot jumps, tilting its perch, upsetting a bag of seeds into a bucket. The bucket drops and pulls a cord, lighting a cigar lighter, setting off a skyrocket. This causes a sickle to cut a string, causing a pendulum with a napkin attached to swing back and forth, wiping Professor Butt's chin. The self-operating napkin features in a cartoon by Rube Goldberg, famous for his complex devices that perform the simplest tasks in highly convoluted ways.

Is this where we are with the golf swing? Have we created a hugely complex swing, when in reality it's much simpler? It seems strange that we add ever-more layers of detail and complexity, believing that we'll somehow make it easier to perform. For example, in a recent TV programme, a well-known coach explained the 'essential fundamentals of a simple golf swing'. The 15-minute session included over 150 references to body parts, positions, angles and movements. Our problem is that while all these positions undoubtedly occur in a golf swing, humans have no capacity to use them for learning. So while the programme *described* the swing, it had no value in helping us *learn* it. During one golf swing, we might round up one or two 'perfect' positions, but the other 148 will usually escape.

We'll see shortly in Chapter 3 that trying to learn the golf swing as a long sequence of positions conflicts directly with the way humans learn physical skills. We learn best when we think as *little* about technique as possible. We've learnt walking, bike riding, shoelace tying, and thousands of other equally complex skills without knowing anything about their detailed mechanics. And not only have we learnt these skills—we've mastered them. We clearly have innate abilities to master highly complex physical skills. So why do we approach the golf swing so differently?

## The way forward

Golf swing evolution has reached a point where we need to take stock. Swinging a golf club is difficult, but we make it even harder. We've travelled down a high-tech path (admittedly one that is fascinating) without knowing where it would lead. But it's led to confusion and we need an injection of clarity and simplicity.

One way forward would be to extract all the high-quality material from books, magazines, and websites, put it together and create a 'best way to swing'. But we can't do this, because we have no way of identifying high-quality material. Any swing theory or method may or may not be better than the rest; we simply don't know. Unfortunately, the golf swing has existed in an evidence vacuum – we've never had sufficient scientific evidence to support or refute anybody's claims or opinions about how to swing a golf club.

But we're at an exciting juncture. In recent years, a large amount of high-quality research has been published, addressing both golf swing mechanics and effective learning strategies. So for the first time, we can establish a scientifically grounded approach to learning and developing an effective swing.

There's light at the end of the golf swing tunnel.

## Golf swing science

Science works—that's what it's for. When we want to know the facts about something, we use science to find them. Science works by continually rejecting false ideas and opinions, to take us progressively closer to the truth. So we can be confident that well-conducted, highly scrutinised research gets close to the truth about the golf swing. Scientists start with an opinion – a hypothesis – that they test rigorously, to the stage where they can accept it as fact. Only when the original opinion has been scientifically proven, is it considered fit for purpose. Science is, in effect, the process of selecting explanations that make fewest assumptions, discarding explanations that lack evidence, and replacing information based on opinion with information based on fact.

We can now do this for the golf swing, but many of us shy away from grappling with science, because we feel it's too complex and we won't understand the concepts or the jargon. And we may be right – for non-scientists, science *is* hard to understand. Also, the golf swing is itself highly complex – a three-dimensional movement, involving virtually every limb and muscle in the body, controlled by a sophisticated brain-body communication system. The laws of physics and the limits of human physiology control its mechanics; the human brain controls execution. Faced with such a complex movement, analysed with complex science, of course we shy away.

But fortunately, we can make it simple – we can translate the science into a language we can all understand. In fact, an important principle of science is that scientists should *always* simplify things. This book does that. The complexities and jargon of the underlying science have already been dealt with, high-quality research findings have been extracted, synthesised, and interpreted, and the results are presented in our language.

The book is based on research findings selected from more than 200 scientific articles, collected from the fields of physics, biomechanics and physiology (how the golf swing works), together with psychology and neuroscience (how to learn it). It may be surprising that such a wide range of sciences are relevant to swinging a golf club, but it demonstrates that the golf swing is more than just a mechanics problem. If we want a better swing, we not only need to understand the mechanics, but also how those mechanics are controlled. We need a *multidisciplinary* approach to understanding and learning an effective golf swing.

This approach is common in other sports. Modern-day, high-performance sport typically involves not only coaches, but also support teams of scientists drawn from many fields, who continually scan the scientific horizon, seeking new information that can push the boundaries of performance in their sports. In doing this, they maximise the performance of elite athletes and optimise the effectiveness of coaching at all levels.

This book adopts the same approach – it's a multidisciplinary analysis of the best way to *improve* a golf swing, combining effective swing mechanics and effective learning strategies. And luckily, the science shows that the simplest approach is best.

## TAKEAWAYS

⟋ Golf swing complexity is a major barrier to learning.

⟋ A multidisciplinary, scientific analysis will identify the best way to learn and develop an effective golf swing.

⟋ Knowing *how to learn* a physical skill is at least as important as knowing the *mechanics* of the skill.

# Part 2
# How we learn

*There are, of course, hundreds more faults in driving which it is possible to commit, but I have no desire to turn the beginner into that most miserable creature, a fault-searching maniac ….*

—Bernard Darwin[3]

# 3

# Survival skills

**M**OST OF US want to improve our golf swings. And we can, because we possess sophisticated biological systems for learning and mastering physical skills. Within each of us lies the innate, but mostly dormant, ability to develop an effortless, powerful, and accurate golf swing.

Unfortunately, few of us ever develop such a swing—we must be doing something wrong. To discover what that something is, we need to understand exactly how we learn physical skills. Armed with this knowledge, we can then set about improving our golf swings in a more effective way.

It's important that we consider *how* we learn before we tackle *what* to learn. If we don't, there's a danger we'll try to learn all the wrong things. So in this section, we'll investigate our innate, biological skill-learning mechanisms. And the best place to start is the subconscious coaching methods of Ernest Jones.

## Learning subconsciously

Ernest Jones was a successful golf swing coach of the early- and mid-20th century, famous for his *whole swing* approach to coaching. He criticised the tendency of swing coaches to divide the swing into numerous parts, comparing it to dissecting a cat. He described the process as producing 'blood, guts, and bones all over the place—but no cat'.

His views were born out of an unfortunate personal experience. Shortly after becoming a professional golfer, World War I interrupted his career and while he was fighting in France, an exploding grenade removed the lower half of his right leg. He returned to England and, after four months recuperation, he tried to play a round of golf. Walking on crutches and swinging on one leg, he scored 83. Within weeks, he'd scored 72.

This episode changed Jones's approach to swing coaching. He initially couldn't understand how his swing could remain highly effective even though he was missing an important limb. He concluded that the human brain, faced with a new physical challenge, could devise compensating strategies that continue to produce the desired outcome, using a modified technique. He believed the brain, knowing only the desired result, could develop an effective technique without any conscious input from its owner. In other words, the golfer's only conscious task is to decide the *outcome*; the brain then decides subconsciously *how to achieve it*.

Ernest Jones adapted his coaching methods to reflect this belief. Instead of requiring his pupils to focus on body parts and positions, he asked them to focus on the clubhead. He reasoned that the golf swing's most important element is the clubhead – and where it travels – so it's best to focus on that. The brain will work out exactly how to make it travel accurately. He explained these principles in his book *Swing the Clubhead* (1937). He became one of the most successful swing coaches of his era, despite a rejection from the coaching establishment because his methods were 'too simple' and 'wouldn't sell enough lessons'.

Ernest Jones, without knowing it, had stumbled across *implicit learning* – the ability of humans (and all animals) to learn skills subconsciously.[4] He didn't call it that, of course, but his reasoning amounted to the same thing. Humans learn all their physical skills implicitly; we learn skills best when we focus on *what* to achieve, not on *how* to achieve it.

Implicit learning has its roots in evolution. Humans and animals have survived over millennia in a dangerous world by subconsciously learning the many skills needed to survive. The young cat learns mouse-catching skills by focusing on the mouse; humans chased and hunted animals in the same way. In today's safer world, we learn to reach for, grasp, and drink a cup of coffee by focusing on the cup, then the mouth. We don't require any knowledge of technique.

Implicit learning has two remarkable qualities. First, it's a truly subconscious process; it just happens. Second, once we've learnt a skill implicitly, we don't know what we've learnt – we know we *can* do it, but we don't know *how* we do it. Our bodies follow the Nike motto: they 'just do it'. But for the golf swing, the opposite applies—we know everything about *what* to do, but we can't do it.

## Dynamic interactions

We can now begin to see why treating the golf swing as a purely mechanical 'joints and levers' problem – and trying to learn it that way – is ineffective. It's because we're using *conscious* mental processes to force our joints and levers to move in certain ways, rather than allowing *subconscious* processes to work it all out. Our problem is that human brains have extremely limited conscious processing capacity, so taking a joints and levers approach to the swing massively exceeds our mental capabilities. Unfortunately, there are simply too many joints and levers – our primitive infor-mation-processing systems simply can't cope. That's why we have such powerful, subconscious, *implicit* systems.

In order to develop an effective golf swing, we need to take a new approach, replacing our conscious efforts to make things happen with strategies to let things happen. In doing this, we'll allow our implicit skill-learning systems to do their work, instead of stifling them. When we allow our implicit systems to work in this way, we not only engage our motor systems (joints and lev-ers), but we also recruit our perceptual, cognitive, respiratory and circulatory systems. We develop a *dynamic interaction* of all our biological control systems. This sounds difficult, but actually, it's easier—we no longer need to *make* so many things happen.

We can see why we need this approach when we consider the control processes operating during a golf swing. To make a swing, the brain sends a stream of neurological signals – a *signal package* – throughout the nervous system to numerous muscle groups. The signals trigger a highly complex, coordinated package of muscle contractions—the swing. Working backwards through the system, if we want an improved golf swing downstream, we need to im-prove the signals sent out upstream, by our brains. We need to address the *cause* of the swing, not the swing itself (the effect). So the key to a better swing is to *think better thoughts.*

Experts in skill development no longer analyse sports skills solely in terms of their mechanics. They adopt a *dynamic systems*[5] approach, where they study mechanical movements *in relation to the other biological systems that control them.* Instead of seeing the human body just as a collection of moving parts, they see it as a sophisticated, multisystem, highly adaptable organism, capable of learning and mastering the most complex of physical skills. The essential point with respect to our golf swings is that humans are good at learning *skills*, not positions. A thousand 'correct positions', even when achieved 'perfectly', won't make a skill. But a well-learned skill can create a thousand correct positions. Unfortunately, in the golf swing, we've confused the two.

We should now consider exactly how implicit learning works, because this holds the key to our golf swing improvement. Just how do we master a complex skill with no conscious effort? We do it through *repetition*.

## Repetition, repetition, repetition

Cats and humans hone their mouse-catching and coffee-drinking skills through repeated attempts to achieve the desired result. They improve their skills through *practice*. Improvement through practice follows a distinct pattern. When we first attempt a new skill, we usually fail. We see the results and we try again. For this next attempt, our brains reorganise and produce an improved signal package. With each repeated attempt, our brains send out newly modified packages that generate movements more appropriate to grasping coffee cups or swinging golf clubs. We improve, and in time, we become experts; we spill no coffee, or we make an effective golf swing.

We can see this in the cat. The young cat – still at the novice mouse-catching stage – formulates a plan (catch that mouse). The plan triggers a movement (a chase and a pounce). There's a result, which at first doesn't match the original plan (the mouse escapes). The cat's brain registers the discrepancy between the plan and the result (feedback) and subconsciously reorganises to produce an improved set of movements next time. Repetition progressively reduces the error between the plan and the result, so that eventually the mouse is caught. The cat's brain works *subconsciously* with its other biological systems to master the skill. The cat knows nothing about mouse-catching technique. But it perfects one— implicitly.

## Swing signatures

Implicit learning has a further quality that's important for our golf swings. All animals, including humans, arrive at different *movement solutions* to any physical problem. Not all cats chase and pounce identically. To us, their movements may look alike (because they're all cats), but they develop different techniques. Their techniques vary because cats themselves vary, in terms of size, speed, visual acuity and many other things. So they develop different movement solutions for catching mice. The 'perfect mouse-catching technique' doesn't exist.

Humans also differ, so left to our own devices we'll also develop different movement solutions to our problem of hitting golf balls – we'll develop unique *swing signatures*. The point is, as long as we practise our individual swing solutions – whatever they look like – implicit learning will ensure they become effective. They'll be our own best movement solutions. So the 'perfect golf swing' – a single, mechanically pure sequence of movements that's best for everyone – can't exist. It can't be the best solution for everyone, simply because we're all different. All swings need to adhere to some important mechanical principles (Part 3 deals with these), but the small details of technique aren't important.

## The best way to learn

We might at this point consider two important questions. First, most top golfers have been heavily coached, and their coaching probably included instructions to focus *explicitly* on many positions, angles and movements. And these players are good! So surely, doesn't explicit learning also work? Second, if we learn best through implicit learning, can we use our vast, detailed knowledge of golf swing mechanics to improve upon it?

The answer to the first question is yes. If we hit thousands of golf balls focusing explicitly on technique, we'll certainly improve. But we can't say for sure that achieving any specific technique actually caused the improvement. It's more likely the many thousands of repetitions caused it. In other words, swing improvement may have occurred *in spite of*, not because of, the technique focus. In fact, we'll see in Chapter 4 that focusing on technique actually *hinders* learning.

The answer to the second question is also yes. We shouldn't ignore technique completely (at least half this book is about technique). The point is, we need to establish the optimum balance between maximising the power of our implicit learning processes and supporting them with an appropriate (that is, *small*) amount of technique. We'll achieve this if we view golf swing mechanics as a small number of big movements – big swing *chunks* – rather than an endless list of small ones. And if we can link them with some simple swing thoughts – that won't overload our primitive thinking capacities – we'll have created the best way to learn. Our brains will have the right amount of information, presented in the right way, with which to work.

The key to this process is our thoughts. Our swing thoughts are the upstream cause of all our good and bad swings, so controlling our thoughts is the key to controlling swing mechanics. Our final task in Part 2 therefore, is to enter – briefly – the mysterious world of *human memory*.

## TAKEAWAYS

ℐ We learn, develop and master physical skills subconsciously (implicitly), without any need to achieve a specific technique.

ℐ Trying to learn the golf swing as a series of positions massively overloads our limited conscious processing capacity and hinders learning.

ℐ The golf swing is a dynamic, subconscious interplay of many biological systems.

ℐ Subconscious learning takes place through repetition – we improve through *practice*.

# 4

# Human memory

IN A WELL-KNOWN CHILDREN'S NURSERY RHYME, a toad asks a centipede how it coordinates its 100 legs. The centipede thinks about it, can't work it out, becomes confused, and falls into a ditch; it can no longer walk. Much the same happens to golfers – thinking about how we swing a golf club confuses us. The human brain has many powerful attributes, but unfortunately, thinking isn't one of them. We think with our memories, and they're rather primitive. In this section, we'll discover how thinking about technique during a golf swing actually hinders learning. Our first task is to understand why we don't *need* to think about it.

## In the groove: automaticity

The mechanism by which we produce our golf swings changes as we progress from beginner through to expert. Initially we need to force our swings to happen, but with practice, we can increasingly just allow them to happen. In other words, we *automate* our swings – we progress from active effort to automatic ability. So, how does this change occur?

When we learn any new skill, whether it's the golf swing, walking, shoelace tying, or playing the guitar, we pass through distinct learning stages. Initially, we focus intently on the movements we need to make, consciously trying to control them. For example, when learning a guitar chord we think 'left index finger on the first fret of the second string … middle finger on the third fret …' and so on. We attend carefully to these small, individual movements, trying to make them happen. Our movements are jerky, hesitant, and imprecise; they lack both accuracy and fluidity.

But with repeated attempts, we improve. Our movements become smoother, faster, and more accurate. Individual movements gradually merge into larger movement *chunks* (chords). The chunks themselves become *chained* (chord sequences), in a more fluid and effortless movement. Our hands and fingers eventually move subconsciously from chord to chord. At this stage, we've automated the skill and filed it away in our brains, from where we can call it up and run it off automatically, as required.

The important point – crucial to our golf swings – is that these automated skills operate best when they run off *without any conscious attention from us*. We no longer need to think about them, or check the achievement of intermediate stages. In fact, we mustn't do this, because it destroys our hard-won automaticity. So in the golf swing, (except, as we'll see, for beginners), thinking about positions only serves to disrupt the swing – trying to make a good swing happen actually stops it happening.

But most of us spend an extravagant amount of time checking and rehearsing one position after another. And, just like the centipede, once we start thinking about things we shouldn't think about, we destroy automaticity, overload our memories, and our golf swings fall into the proverbial ditch. We can no longer swing. The reason focusing consciously on technique has such a damaging effect is that we're using our memories (note the plural) in the wrong way. So what's the right way? In other words, what are our best *swing thoughts*?

## Swing thoughts

Humans have two memories. We have short-term (working) memories that we use for thinking – dealing with the here and now – and long-term memories where we store things. How we use these two memories determines the quality of every golf swing we make. First, we'll consider working memory.

### *Short-term (working) memory*

Working memory holds our current thoughts: what we're conscious of right now. It's a mental scratch pad, where we work out solutions to the next challenge. For example, we use it to calculate if it's safe to cross the road, or to absorb a conversation. When we swing a golf club, this is where we hold our swing thoughts.

It's working memory that has the limited capacity – we can only think consciously about a few things at a time. One of the most quoted papers in psychology has the title: 'The Magical Number Seven – Plus or Minus Two'.[6] The numbers refer to how many items a human can hold in working memory at one time. Subsequent research has revised the figure downwards, from seven to three or four. For many of us, it might be just two, or even one.

So our working memories—have no memory. Specifically, they have no storage capacity. They can *think* in the short term, but they can't *remember*. They certainly can't hold enough information to perform a complex action like the golf swing, which includes thousands of positions. Even if by some miracle, we produce a good swing by working consciously through a long sequence of 'correct' movements, we couldn't repeat them. Yet many of us try to do this; we try to think our way through the swing, moving deliberately through numerous positions.

We see this in beginners, still in their hesitant, working-it-out stages. Beginners *need* to think their way through the swing, because they don't have automated swing routines to rely on. So they're in an impossible position: they have a hundred things to think about, but a thinking capacity that can only handle a few. They stand paralysed over the ball, unable to start. This is 'paralysis by analysis'—and it isn't restricted to beginners.[7]

Luckily, we can overcome the limitations of working memory. As our golf swings achieve automaticity, the neural pathways that control them migrate out of working memory, into *long-term memory*, for storage. And this has a simply vast capacity.

### Long-term memory

Long-term memory is our mental bank, where we store facts, habits, recollections, rules, and the motor patterns for all our physical skills, including our golf swings. We retain these skills for life, hard-wired into our brains. If we need to tie shoelaces, play the guitar, or swing golf clubs, we (subconsciously) delve into this huge skill repository and retrieve a suitable automated routine.

The key point is that when automated routines operate, they *completely bypass conscious, working memory.* This is why we can do one thing and think about another. While subconsciously tying shoelaces, we can consciously run through a checklist of things to take with us when we leave the house. We use each memory appropriately: subconscious, long-term memory for automated shoelace tying, conscious working memory for the possessions check.

So when our golf swings achieve automaticity, our limited working memories become redundant. This is hugely beneficial to our golf swings, but unfortunately, we mostly waste the advantage by deliberately recruiting working memory to think our way through our swings. When we do this, we de-automate the swing – we break it down once more into its numerous components. By interfering in this way, we return to the stage where we need to perform each component separately; we resurrect the hesitant, jerky swings of our beginner days.

As if this wasn't bad enough, thinking about the swing introduces a further problem: not only do we lose fluidity and smoothness, but we also introduce *transition points* between the different swing components. These are sites with high potential for error, which wouldn't appear in the unhindered, automated swing. So overall, thinking our way through the golf swing just doesn't work; trying to do the right thing isn't the right thing to do.[8]

## Trying fails

It's easy to understand why we interfere so much. It's called *trying.* But in complex skills such as the golf swing, trying doesn't work. It's no surprise that we produce our best swings during friendly games, when our conscious thoughts are diverted, and our worst swings during competition, when we're trying. Trying doesn't work because once our swings achieve automaticity, we actually *lose the ability to control them*. So trying to control them is a futile exercise, because at this stage they're beyond our conscious control. Any attempt to produce a swing through conscious thought can't work; it can only disrupt.

Good players excel at this sort of mind control – their minds are cool and focused,[9] attending to relevant things such as the lie, slopes, wind, hazards, and the ball flight. In contrast, the beginner's mind – unable to filter in this way – is awash with random thoughts about slow takeaway, lie, elbows, wind, weight shift, mud on the ball, hip clearance, mustn't slice, and much more.

We can see this in the brainwave activity of beginners and experts during a golf swing. Scientists measure brain activity using electronic traces, with spikier traces indicating higher activity. Beginners show many erratic spikes and haphazard patterns, the neural signature of minds consciously dealing with too many unrelated thoughts. Experts show flatter traces; their minds are calmer. The main danger for experts is if they're tempted – through pressure, for example – to revert to thinking about their swings in an effort to be more careful. This can instantly erase years of practice.

So, to conclude Part 2, the best way to learn the golf swing – the way that maximises the power of implicit learning – is to break it down into as *few* components as possible. This takes full account of how the human brain works and makes maximum use of our most powerful learning systems. Our task in Part 3 is to identify the important swing components (key skills) to learn. We'll see there are just five: four physical skills plus one controlling mental skill.

\\/ \\/ \\/   \\/ \\/ \\/

## TAKEAWAYS

𝟙 How we use our short-term (working) and long-term memories is crucial to making effective golf swings.

𝟙 With practice, our golf swings become automated skill routines, stored in long-term memory, beyond conscious control.

𝟙 Automated swing routines operate most effectively when allowed to run off automatically, without conscious inter-ference from working memory.

𝟙 Thinking our way through our golf swings disrupts automaticity and harms performance.

# Part 3

# The golf swing's five key skills

*There was a time when we hoped that a miracle would occur, and that the dash and strength and glory of hitting which are vouchsafed to the few might suddenly one fine morning descend upon us too, so that we should be as creatures transfigured and made splendid for evermore.*

—Bernard Darwin[10]

# 5

# Preliminaries

F IVE KEY SKILLS – listed below – are essential to making an effective golf swing. Skill 1 is the crucial controlling skill. Skills 2 and 5 determine accuracy. Skills 3–5 determine power.

---

## THE GOLF SWING'S 5 KEY SKILLS

1 An external mental focus

2 An accurate clubhead path through impact

3 A coordinated muscular chain

4 A tight initial downswing radius

5 A passive wrist release.

---

It's worth noting that while reading about these skills may take a few hours, it takes only just over *one second* to perform them. In fact, we need to perform skills 3–5 (and most of skill 2) exclusively during the downswing—which lasts only *two tenths* of a second. The point is that we need to invest time in understanding the skills in order to develop an effective strategy for applying them so quickly.

The list doesn't include the grip, stance, posture, or alignment, for two reasons. First, we have no research to support or refute different versions of any of them. Other texts cover these elements comprehensively and they mostly apply sound mechanical principles. Second, although it's important we get these elements right, we can do it at leisure, before the swing starts. They affect the swing in important ways, but they aren't part of our greater mind-body problem of actually swinging the club.

Also, the backswing isn't discussed separately. This may be surprising, but in any striking skill, the primary purpose of the backswing is to create a height and a distance over which the striking swing can operate. Yes, we need to manoeuvre into a reasonable position from where to make a strike, but as we'll see shortly in Chapter 7, there's no best way to do this. Traditionally, the backswing has been heavily emphasised in golf coaching, reflecting a belief that the golf swing is a fixed, purely mechanical action. This has created a fear that even tiny errors during the early stages of a swing are magnified and irrecoverable during the rest of the swing. But we'll see in Chapter 7 that our sophisticated control systems can cope with variable swing paths.

So now, we can get to grips with the skills themselves. The mental skill comes first, because this is the controlling skill.

# 6

## KEY SKILL 1
## An external mental focus

WILLIAM JAMES, the famous psychologist, advised: 'Keep your eye on the place aimed at, and your hand will fetch it; think of your hand and you will likely miss your aim'.[11] James observed that we perform skills more accurately with a target focus in our minds – focusing *externally* rather than *internally*. And this is at the heart of the eternal golf swing conundrum: why are some of our swings good and others bad, for no apparent reason? The answer lies in our thoughts; we sometimes *think* differently.

When we perform a skill badly, we typically assume the error occurred in our muscles. We look accusingly at some miscreant body part, or rehearse the movement we suspect went wrong. We may even know *what* went wrong, but we don't know *why* it went wrong. It doesn't occur to us that our thoughts caused the bad swing. But it's true: inappropriate thoughts at both the planning and performance stages of a golf swing will disrupt it. It's a sobering thought, but we can seal the fate of any golf swing before a single muscle has started to contract. So in order to make real progress with our golf swings, we need to establish exactly what we should think about before and during each swing.

## Thinking outside the body

Implicit learning starts – as we've seen – with making a plan, so we need to establish the best sort of plan to make for our golf swings. We have a choice: whether to make a plan about how to move, or a plan about what to achieve. And by now, the answer should be clear: we need an *achievement* plan. For many of us, this will be new. We know what a movement plan looks like (read any coaching book), but what is an achievement plan? As the name suggests, it involves focusing on a desired outcome.

We have evidence from many sports and activities that players who mentally focus on objects or images outside their bodies outperform players who focus on technique.[12] In other words, an *external* focus is better than an *internal* focus. This has been found in basketball, distance running, darts, high jump, long jump, rifle shooting, soccer, tennis, weightlifting, and volleyball—even pedalling a pedalo. Performers in high-skill activities outside sport can also benefit from an external focus. Patients physically disabled through stroke or Parkinson's disease recover movement skills faster using exercises that encourage a target focus. Surgeons who adopt an external focus can devote more attention to nontechnical tasks, minimising the effects of surgical stress. So what are the best external thoughts to have for our golf swings?

In other sports, the answer is obvious. The darts player will focus on the dartboard; the basketball shooter will focus on the ring; the cricketer and baseball batter will focus on the ball. In golf, we've a choice. We might focus on the planned ball trajectory, or the target area. Alternatively, we can focus on the ball, or the clubhead path through impact. The essential point is that we need to train our working memories to hold external thoughts and images that don't interfere with the automatic operation of our swings.

Many sports have replaced highly technical coaching with simpler approaches. In swimming, instructions such as 'high elbow, fingertips first, reach forward from the shoulder, don't cross the centre line, and roll the body 60 degrees', have been replaced with 'pull the water past you'. To make fast turns, swimmers just think about 'hot walls'. In races, they may focus on 'easy speed'. In basketball, coaches tell players to 'reach for the cookie in the cookie jar', to encourage good shooting technique. Tennis players learn the drop volley shot by imagining they're turning a key in a lock. These simple, external images and analogies are highly effective in encouraging skill learning. Although a huge amount of science is raising sports performance to new heights, at the level of the athlete it's translated into simpler concepts.

Scientists have conducted numerous experiments to establish the most effective mental focus for the golf swing. Researchers typically divide golfers into groups, giving each group different instructions. They will instruct one group to focus on some aspect of technique. They might instruct a second group to think about a holistic cue word, such as 'rhythm' or 'smooth'. And they might tell a third group simply to 'try to hit the ball as close to the target as possible'. Sometimes, researchers tell a group to think of something completely irrelevant, such as a colour. Or they might ask them to count backwards from 100, or to sing a song.

The clear and consistent message from these experiments is that whereas complete beginners do benefit from focusing on technique, everyone else performs better focusing on the cue words, the target, or the irrelevant thoughts and images. The holistic cue word seems to work best. Results are most striking when researchers apply pressure to the players, usually in the form of offering a cash prize, or telling the players their performances will be recorded. Here, we have our first clue that an external focus also protects us during high-pressure moments, as we'll see in the next section.

## Grace under pressure

After 72 holes of the 1989 US Masters tournament, Scott Hoch and (now Sir) Nick Faldo were tied for the lead. On the first sudden-death hole, Hoch had a straight, two-foot putt to win. He pulled the ball left; it never touched the hole. Faldo won. Three years later, in the Open Championship at Muirfield, Nick Faldo started the final round leading, but midway through the round, he started dropping shots and lost the lead. He told himself to 'forget everything', 'clear the mind', and 'play on automatic'. He trusted his swing, played exceptional golf under immense pressure, and won.[13] Scott Hoch probably succumbed to *choking* – when under pressure, he failed to perform at the expected level. Faldo achieved 'grace under pressure', the phrase Ernest Hemmingway coined to describe fortitude. He didn't choke.

We usually think of choking as our nerves getting the better of us, causing us to become jittery and lose muscular control. Or we might believe thoughts of winning or the consequences of failure distract us from the task in hand. These things may happen, but the main cause of choking is our minds wandering internally to-wards technique, trying to be extra careful. We try to make sure we get the technique exactly right – but this is the worst thing we can do.

Pressure doesn't cause a bad shot by distracting us, it does so by tempting us to try to apply too much *control*. A golf swing un-der pressure looks 'steery', because the player is trying to steer the ball carefully, searching for extra control. The swing looks – and is – slower and more deliberate than usual. The player is once again thinking through the movements, running off components sepa-rately. The swing has become more beginner-like; it's been de-automated.

Interestingly, beginners don't choke. Because they already *need* to attend consciously to technique, doing so under pressure isn't a change for them. In fact, beginners often perform *better* under pressure; trying harder actually works. Similarly, players who have only limited knowledge of swing mechanics perform better under pressure – they can't think about things they don't know. Learning the golf swing naturally – without an excess of tech-nique-focused coaching – may be the best way to pressure-proof a golf swing.

Fortunately, choking has a remedy. We can train ourselves to maintain an external focus when we swing under pressure. Like Nick Faldo, we can learn to clear all technique-related thoughts from our minds and trust our golf swing autopilots. For pressure situations, we need to develop the Nike 'just do it' mentality. Lee Trevino is one of the best examples of a pressure-proofed golfer. Spectators thought he was crazy to continue talking to the crowd as he walked up to the ball and took his swing, even in high-pressure situations. Yet talking to the crowd occupied his mind, so he couldn't use his working memory to interfere with his automated swing routine. PGA tour professional Toney Penna once commented that everyone has two swings: their normal swing and a swing they bring out for the last three holes. We all have a last three holes swing, but thinking correctly will keep it under control. Chapter 14 contains some practical examples of external swing images and thoughts we can use in our golf swings.

## The pink elephant

One final benefit of an external focus is that it's a positive strategy; it's something to *do,* rather than something to *avoid.* If someone tells us 'don't think of a pink elephant'—we immediately think of a pink elephant. We do this because our brains first need to process the pink elephant image, before they can understand the don't instruction. In golf, the thought 'don't hook it out-of-bounds' immediately creates a mental image of the ball hooking out-of-bounds. So a hook out-of-bounds signal package formulates in the brain. Unfortunately, golf can involve too many pink elephants.[14]

## Takeaways

*I* An internal mental focus (thinking about technique) disrupts a swing's automaticity.

*I* An external (outside the body) mental focus allows automated skill routines to run off unhindered.

*I* A holistic cue word is the most effective external focus.

*I* An external focus makes a golf swing more robust under pressure.

# 7

## KEY SKILL 2
# An accurate clubhead path through impact

J AMES BRUEN was born in Belfast in 1920. His first junior handicap was six and by age 15, it was plus one. He captained the Great Britain and Ireland Walker Cup team while still a teenager. His mere presence on the victorious 1938 team is reputed to have both inspired his own team and terrified the American opposition, because of his immense power and shot-making ability. His peers rated him the greatest player in the world, amateur or professional.

We might presume James Bruen had a perfect golf swing, but in fact, he swung the club in an enormous loop—the infamous Bruen Loop. At the top of his backswing, his club shaft pointed not down the target line, but at the tee box.[15] Would James Bruen have been a better player without his loop? We'll never know of course, but his extraordinary swing and wonderful ball striking skills must again cast doubt on the concept of a single, perfect way to swing a golf club.

In this section, we're concerned with controlling the whole swing. We need to establish the best way of manoeuvring the clubhead throughout its 8-metre journey, disappearing out of sight, changing direction, yet travelling (briefly) along the target line at impact. To discover the best way to do this, we need to start with the observations of Sir Karl Popper.

# Of clocks and clouds

Sir Karl Popper, the scientific philosopher, proposed that most things in the world resemble either clocks or clouds. Clocks are neat, orderly systems, easily explained by studying their predictable mechanics. Clouds, on the other hand, are a mess: irregular, disorderly, and unpredictable. Popper suggested that it's a mistake to pretend everything in the world is a clock. Yet we do it all the time. We like logical, orderly, mechanical things that we can explain scientifically through maths and physics. So we love clocks. Faced with a cloud, our first instinct is to see it as a clock.

We do this with the golf swing. We narrow our eyes and we see the laws of physics clearly at work; it *looks* like a clock. So, we conclude, it must *be* a clock. But we forget that a human brain is in control; to most of us, our golf swings *feel* like extremely disorderly and unpredictable *clouds*. The problem is, trying to explain the golf swing as a clock, when it's controlled by one of the most unpredictable, cloud-like objects in the world (us), won't help us learn effective swings. Also, it tempts us to work out the 'best' mechanical way to swing and to call it 'the perfect swing'. But does it really exist?

# The perfect golf swing

Experienced blacksmiths strike the hot iron with great accuracy. Their hammerhead paths, as they home in on their targets, are virtually identical. But despite having perfect hammerhead control, blacksmiths have different swing techniques – they perform different body movements to achieve similarly accurate strikes. And not only do techniques differ *between* blacksmiths, they also differ *within* blacksmiths. Each individual blacksmith performs different body movements in each swing they make, yet always achieves an accurate strike. In blacksmithing, the 'perfect blacksmith's hammer swing' doesn't exist.[16]

We see the same in shooting. Expert shooters control their gun barrels by coordinating the movements of their wrist, elbow, and shoulder joints. Their joint movements vary constantly, but muscular coordination ensures a high level of control. Again, the shooters aim perfectly, but a 'perfect shooting technique' doesn't exist.[17]

In golf, we take the opposite approach – we believe in the perfect golf swing.[18] We believe we can artificially force our bodies through an intricate series of predetermined, perfect positions. We've already seen this induces an internal focus, but it has another – equally damaging – effect. When we constrain our swings into a fixed movement, we override our powerful, subconscious control systems; we nullify our ability to learn implicitly.

The explanation is simple. Maintaining dynamic control over a hammer, gun or golf club relies on our joints having *freedom of movement*. When joints are free to move, they can coordinate and apply the highest levels of control. But if we constrain our swings into a fixed set of positions and movements, we remove this freedom and effectively stifle our main control weapon. So like the blacksmiths and shooters, we need to allow our body movements to vary when we swing. In this way, our swings will develop the two important qualities lacking in constrained swings: they'll become *adaptable* and *self-correcting*.[19]

We've known for a long time that in any sport, efforts to control one part of a complex movement always have unintended and unpredictable effects on other parts. So constraining one or more elements of our swings to operate in a particular way simply disrupts other elements. It's an endless task – like trying to pack too many clothes into a suitcase. As soon as we fix one corner, clothes bulge out everywhere else.

Allowing variability and freedom of movement in our swings not only fits well with human skill-learning theory, but it's also supported by evidence of improved performance. Players with the most variable swings produce the most consistent shots[20] – variable, adaptable, self-correcting swings clearly work better than fixed, constrained swings. This is the opposite of the received golf wisdom, which views swing variability as a problem, which needs to be coached out.

So the important message is that in order to achieve an accurate clubhead through impact, we need to focus on—an accurate clubhead path through impact! Focusing on the outcome is the surest way to achieve it, because it allows our bodies freedom of movement to exert fine control. We can be relatively relaxed about the specific clubhead path during the backswing – there's time to self-correct – but we need to be increasingly conscious of accuracy as the clubhead approaches impact. In other words, achieving an accurate clubhead path through impact is a progressive, 'rounding up of the clubhead' exercise, not a robotic, position-to-position procedure.

One further dimension of the perfect golf swing deserves a brief mention: whether a swing needs to *look* perfect. Even a cursory glance at top players' swings tells us that many techniques can be highly effective. And this shouldn't surprise us, because we all learn our swings under different sets of *limitations*.[21] Unique combinations of age, gender, fitness, physique, flexibility, weather conditions, practice facilities, and available equipment dictate how our swings develop. In time, our swings stabilise, as we learn to minimise effort and maximise performance. All our swings work, but they look – and are – different.

So not only do our swings vary each time we swing, they're also different from everybody else's. This means the perfect swing may have an infinite number of guises—one for each of us. Many people consider that Ben Hogan's swing was close to perfect, but it was probably only perfect for Ben Hogan. Lee Trevino didn't have a Hogan-like swing – far from it – but he probably had the perfect swing for Lee Trevino.

## The corridor of certainty

To help develop an unconstrained swing, we can organise our thoughts around a *swing corridor* – a clubhead path with a margin of error around it. Within this corridor, we can be confident that our subconscious control systems will iron out any deviations, effectively rounding up the clubhead towards impact.

In cricket, players refer to the 'corridor of uncertainty' – a target zone within which bowlers try to bowl the ball.[22] Any ball landing inside this zone induces uncertainty in the batsman's mind. So maybe there's a golf equivalent – a corridor of *certainty* – a swing zone within which the clubhead can rove around at will, without overstretching our self-correcting mechanisms. This fits well with our knowledge of how the human body works.

Viewing the golf swing as a naturally variable movement doesn't conflict with the concept of an automated swing. Automaticity doesn't mean fixed; an automated swing can still adapt. In fact, the opposite applies – automaticity and adaptability *depend on each other*. If we lose one, we lose both.

But we should be a little cautious. We may be unwise to think we can swing the club anywhere and everything will be OK. The corridor may not be *that* wide. Some positions in the golf swing may be important landmarks that we *do* need to achieve. For example, top players reproduce their top of the backswing positions consistently from swing to swing. At this moment though, it isn't clear how important this might be.

## Controllable chaos

We can think of a variable golf swing as 'controllable chaos'[23] – a term used to describe effective biological control systems. It's well known that the ability of joints to move freely is *essential* to achieving precise control over a complex movement. This calls into question the fixed view of the golf swing, in which any tiny deviation is believed to set off an unstoppable sequence of magnified errors through the rest of the swing.

Thinking that the swing should be fixed suggests a belief in the 'butterfly effect', a concept originally proposed by Edward Lorenz. Lorenz was a meteorologist who entered the same data twice into a computer program to forecast the weather. But the computer program produced radically different forecasts from the same data. Lorenz discovered one set of numbers had been rounded down from six decimal places to three. The size of the error was negligible, but the computer program magnified it, producing completely different forecasts. This incident gave rise to Lorenz's famous lecture: 'Does the flap of a butterfly's wing in Brazil set off a tornado in Texas?'[24] A belief in the butterfly effect is the reason we agonise so much over that first movement from the ball – we're desperate to make it perfect, fearful of the consequences of a small mistake.

An additional – and immensely satisfying – benefit of a variable golf swing is that it stops us worrying about swing plane. We agonise a lot about swing plane. We've read about the shaft plane, hand plane, hip plane, shoulder plane, clubhead plane, arm plane, ball-buckle plane, ball-shoulder plane, single-plane, two-plane, plane of glass, D plane—and more. But whichever plane we choose – and they all exist in the golf swing – it can only have two dimensions, because a plane has no thickness. So trying to fit a variable, three-dimensional swing into any two-dimensional swing plane model isn't useful. While having a mental image of a swing plane can help us marshal our swing thoughts (see Chapter 14), we needn't worry about whether we actually achieve it—we won't. Accepting that our clubheads will wander – in fact, *should* wander – rescues us from the swing plane jungle.

A further benefit is that an adaptable, self-correcting swing is a better weapon on the golf course. Most shots we face demand something slightly different from our swings: subtle variations in clubhead path, angle of attack, and clubface angle. An adaptable, self-correcting swing is better able to deliver subtlety.

So now, we have an uncomplicated and relatively stress-free way of developing an accurate clubhead path through impact. But some bad news lurks just around the corner. The reason we need an accurate clubhead path is to hit the ball straight. But with modern equipment, clubhead path determines only around *15 per cent* of the initial ball flight direction. And in low-friction conditions (for example, when water or grass come between the ball and the clubface), it's as little as *five* per cent. The clubface *angle* at impact determines the remaining 85–95 per cent.[25] We'll cover this in Chapter 10 – our more immediate task is to inject some effortless power into the swing.

## TAKEAWAYS

*I* We can produce an accurate clubhead path through impact via an infinite variety of coordinated joint and lever movements.

*I* There's little scientific support for the concept of a single, 'perfect golf swing'.

*I* We all swing differently, depending on our personal set of learning limitations.

*I* Our golf swings vary from swing to swing and this is healthy, because unconstrained swings are adaptable and self-correcting.

# 8

## KEY SKILL 3
# A coordinated muscular chain

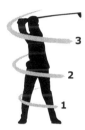

WE ALL CRAVE EFFORTLESS POWER, the hallmark of the top player. But, for many of us, it's a mystery how those effortless swings accelerate the clubhead from zero to over 100 miles per hour in just two tenths of a second. But it's no mystery; we know exactly how it happens. And we all have the ability to do it. The next three chapters explain how. First, consider the big picture: we'll generate effortless power if we achieve three things:

- *Muscular coordination,* to drive body rotation and generate rotational speed
- *Low rotational resistance,* to maximise rotational speed
- *A passive wrist release,* to convert rotational speed into maximum clubhead speed.

This section is concerned with the first skill – muscular coordination.

## Power and speed

Let's clear up a misconception. The key to a powerful golf swing isn't muscular power; it's muscular *coordination.* Although we talk about a 'powerful' swing, it's a bit of a misnomer; we don't need big, strong muscles. Also, the concept of power in the golf swing can itself be confusing. We may have read explanations of power that include scientific terms such as force, work, torque, velocity (linear and angular), and energy. They're important, but most of us don't fully understand what they are or how they relate to each other, so we never really grasp where golf swing power comes from, or even what it is.

Here, we'll adopt a simpler approach. We'll focus on the one thing we know we simply *have* to achieve—*speed.* Clubhead speed is the primary determinant of how far we hit the ball, so our downswings have to generate speed. The first stage in achieving high speed in the downswing is to generate *rotational speed* in our bodies as they unwind. And the most effective and efficient way to achieve rotational speed is to use a range of muscle groups, all working in perfect harmony. We need a *coordinated muscular chain.*[26]

## The chain

The muscular chain starts at our feet and works in an upward and outward direction through our legs, hips, trunk, shoulders, and finally our arms and club. At the start of the downswing, we push against the ground with our leg muscles to start hip rotation. Our hips accelerate and then slow down. This braking action transfers the speed to the next link in the chain, the trunk. The trunk picks up the speed and activates the shoulder turn, generating even more speed. This *combined* rotational speed of hips and shoulders is far higher than either muscle group could generate acting alone.

The key point is that we *accumulate* speed through the length of the chain. Each link receives speed, adds to it, and passes it on to the next. Speed *flows* along the chain, multiplying at each link. The chain is effective only if each muscle group plays a *proportional* – not a dominant – part. Correct sequencing is crucial – muscles early in the chain (legs and trunk) start the sequence and must work gradually; muscles later in the chain (shoulders and arms) must wait.

An important feature of the process is efficient speed transfer between the links. The mechanism for transferring speed is the braking action of each link. We can see this in slow motion videos, where each moving link – the hips, shoulders, and hands – slows visibly at the point where the next link takes over. The hands are the easiest to see – they slow down markedly just before impact, becoming a pivot point around which the club rotates. Sometimes the chain breaks down. Particular problems arise when a muscle group dominates by working too strongly, or by working out of turn. For example, we might hit with our arms. Hitting simply activates the arms prematurely – it destroys the chain and speed leaks away.

So how can we develop a coordinated muscular chain? It's important to recognise that only a few milliseconds separate each set of muscle contractions, so we can't really control it. The muscular chain is an immensely complex package of muscular contractions that we can *only* learn *implicitly*. We can't learn it through positions. Our best strategy is to develop a sense of our bodies working sequentially in an upwards and outwards direction – a sort of anticlockwise, corkscrewing action. A coordinated muscular chain will *emerge* over time. Our main danger is failing to appreciate how the muscular chain works – or that it even exists – so we never try to develop it. Chapter 14 includes some swing thoughts to develop a coordinated muscular chain.

One of the best examples of a muscular chain operating in sport is a Roger Federer tennis serve. His preparation puts his body in an excellent, coiled, striking position, and then the chain unwinds seamlessly, from his feet to the racquet head – effortless power.

So what sort of muscular engine do we need to drive our muscular chains? We don't need massive power, so a Ferrari would be extravagant. On the other hand, an ageing Trabant couldn't cope. Our golf swings need a mid-range motor in which all the parts work smoothly and reliably together: obviously, we need a VW Golf.

## TAKEAWAYS

ꟾ We generate rotational speed through a *coordinated muscular chain*.

ꟾ Muscular work follows an upward and outward sequence starting from our legs, flowing through our hips and shoulders and finishing with our arms.

ꟾ We accumulate speed throughout the length of the chain, with each link playing a proportional, not dominant, part.

ꟾ The chain relies on correct sequencing and coordination of muscular contractions – the chain breaks down if a segment tries to dominate.

ꟾ We don't need a Ferrari.

# *9*

## Key skill 4
# A tight initial downswing radius

A COORDINATED MUSCULAR CHAIN is only half the battle for rotational speed. We also have to ensure that when we apply the turning force, our efforts meet as little *resistance* as possible. Maximum force, combined with minimum resistance generates maximum speed. To discover how we can minimise rotational resistance, we need to understand the remarkable balancing feats of Jean François Gravelet (Charles) Blondin.

### Blondin makes an omelette

In 1859, Charles Blondin walked a tightrope across the Niagara Falls, pushing a wheelbarrow containing a stove. He stopped halfway, lit the stove, and cooked an omelette. He lowered the omelette to passengers watching from the boat *Maid of the Mist,* in the river below. Blondin then packed up his stove and completed his crossing successfully. Blondin made this task easier by carrying a long pole, which had the effect of slowing down any sideways rotation (loss of balance), allowing him time to recover. We experience the same effect when we cross a stream using a narrow plank – we instinctively hold our arms out to the side, because it helps us stay in balance. Like Blondin, we increase our *rotational resistance*.

We can explain this effect quite simply. When a rotational force (gravity for Blondin, muscular chain for us) acts on an object, a larger, heavier, extended object will have more rotational resistance and hence rotate slower than a smaller, lighter, compact object. The resistance is greater if the weight is located well away from the object's centre, so a long, heavy pole is perfect for tightrope walking.

Rotational resistance – and therefore rotational speed – changes whenever body shape changes. For example, a figure skater can start a slow spin with arms outstretched and then spin faster by pulling their arms in close to their body. They make no additional effort; they just make themselves smaller. In Blondin's case, his pole made him both heavier and bigger, and distributed the weight away from his body. Each of these slowed rotation. On our plank, our extended arms don't make us heavier, but they do make us bigger and distribute our weight away from our bodies, so we also slow rotation.

The same forces that kept Blondin on his wire and us on our plank stop us hitting long drives. We'll also slow rotation if we increase resistance by allowing our long pole – the club – to stick out. We want the opposite – fast rotation – so we need to keep it tucked in. The key to reducing resistance and maximising rotational speed is to maintain a *tight initial downswing radius*. Swing

radius is simply the distance between the swing's hub (somewhere near the centre of the chest) and the clubhead. It's smallest
at the top of the backswing (position A, in Figure 1), because
we've brought the clubhead in close to the hub by hinging our
wrists. And it's highest at address and impact because our arms
are fully extended and in a straight line with the club (C). So the
key skill is to keep a tight swing radius during the first part of the
downswing (from A to B), when our muscular chains are driving
rotation.

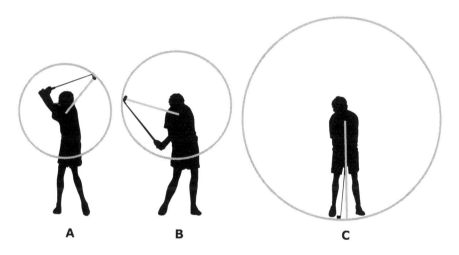

Figure 1. *Swing radius at three stages of the downswing*

The way we maintain a tight swing radius is by keeping our
wrists fully hinged – lagging the clubhead. We can see why this is
such a crucial feature of an effective golf swing—it increases rotational speed. In the previous chapter, we said that our muscular
chains generate rotational speed, but we should have added '… as
long as we don't slow things down by allowing the clubhead to
escape from its tight radius'. Chapter 14 contains some simple
swing thoughts to help us achieve a tight swing radius.

So now, we've considered the two key skills required to generate rotational speed: a coordinated muscular chain combined with a tight initial downswing radius. It's like driving a car. We have an accelerator (the muscular chain) and a brake (swing radius). We need to press the accelerator and stay off the brake. We call rotational resistance *moment of inertia,* and those who like physics can find a more scientific explanation of how it works in Annex 1.

## TAKEAWAYS

⟋ When a rotational force acts on an object, a smaller, lighter, compact object will rotate faster than a larger, heavier, extended object.

⟋ This is because smaller, lighter, compact objects have lower *rotational resistance*.

⟋ In our golf swings, a tight initial downswing radius makes us smaller and more compact, minimising rotational resistance and maximising *rotational speed*.

⟋ We achieve a tight swing radius by maintaining a full wrist hinge during the initial phase of the downswing.

# 10

## KEY SKILL 5
## A passive wrist release

W E'VE GENERATED HIGH ROTATIONAL SPEED, which now resides in
our arms, and we need to convert it into clubhead speed.
This is the moment where things change dramatically. We convert
an arm speed of around 20 miles per hour into a clubhead speed
of more than 100 miles per hour, in just a fraction of a second. We
only discovered the true source of this massive acceleration relatively recently. In 1972, the *Journal of Dynamic Systems, Measurement, and Control* published a scientific discussion entitled: 'An
obscure influence in the golf shot'. Scientists debated the nature of
forces that could '… bring the clubhead from a position trailing
the shaft to a position abreast of the shaft at impact'.[27]

But even though we haven't always understood the true source
of speed, generations of golfers have understood the skill required
to achieve it: a *passive release of the wrists*. This section explains
how simply allowing the wrists to unhinge creates massive clubhead speed.

# Golf's double pendulum

Speed transfer between our arms and the club happens in essentially the same way as between previous links in the chain, but with one crucial difference. *We don't generate additional speed by applying muscular force to the club.* We derive additional speed by harnessing the power of our hinged, arm-club lever system, which acts as a *double pendulum*. The double pendulum is the obscure influence.

In putting, we're advised to swing our arms and club like a pendulum. We lock our wrists and rock the whole unit around the swing hub, imitating a simple, single pendulum. The full golf swing is this same pendulum, but because our wrists hinge and unhinge, it becomes a double pendulum: one pendulum hanging from another.[28] Figure 2 shows a 'real' double pendulum and the golf version. In the golf version, the first pendulum (the triangle formed by the arms and shoulders) rotates around its hub. The second pendulum (the club) rotates around its hinge (the wrists).

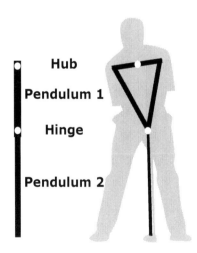

Figure 2. *Real and golf double pendulums*

At address, the double pendulum hangs in its neutral position, with both pendulums aligned vertically. During our backswings, our arms carry the club to a height and we hinge our wrists to around 90 degrees. During the initial phase of the downswing, we hold this hinge angle and we arrive at the position shown in Figure 3. At this point, the double pendulum is prepared to make its powerful strike.

Figure 3. *Double pendulum in the prepared position*

If we arranged a real double pendulum into this position and released it, we would observe a specific sequence of pendulum movements:

- The first pendulum rotates around the hub, accelerating downwards.
- The second pendulum then rotates around the hinge causing the first pendulum to brake.
- The second pendulum overtakes the first pendulum and slingshots through at high speed.[29]

This sequence also occurs in our golf downswings. Our arms accelerate downwards and then brake. The club rotates around our wrists and the clubhead slingshots through at high speed.

The double pendulum has three remarkable properties. First, it generates high speed at the tip of the second pendulum. Second, it generates this speed using only gravity; no other external force is applied. Third, the two pendulums become perfectly synchronised (straightened-out) at the vertical position. Translating these properties into golf swing mechanics, this natural system delivers *high clubhead speed,* for *no additional effort,* and *squares the clubface at impact.* In other words, we get two huge advantages, for simply doing nothing.

Many sports depend on the action of a double pendulum – it's the most efficient way to transfer speed from a heavy body to a lighter implement. It operates in tennis, squash, and badminton shots; the baseball hit; the field hockey shot; darts and javelin throws, and cricket shots. Outside sport, we see it in ringing church bells, moving loads with a crane, and felling trees. The concept of a double pendulum in sport isn't new. In fact, the golf swing is used in physics classes as a practical example of a double pendulum in action. Yet few golfers are aware they have one in their swings, let alone how it works.

We should note that in our golf swings, we do apply force to the first pendulum – we drive our arms with our muscular chains – so our golf swings are essentially *powered double pendulums.* This is OK, because the dynamics don't change. But we mustn't power the second pendulum, the club. This will destroy the system's sensitive dynamics. This final key skill is simply the skill of *allowing* the double pendulum to operate naturally, through a passive wrist release.[30] So now, we know *what* happens, but we still don't know exactly *how* we get all this free speed. It's all to do with the rotation of the earth and roundabouts.

## Free speed

The relative lengths and weights of human arms and the golf club are such that a passive wrist release generates maximum clubhead speed. A passive release simply means we don't have to make it happen – we don't need to search for some magic point in the downswing and then consciously *force* our wrists to unhinge. The process is actually the reverse: powerful forces acting on the clubhead cause it to fly outward and drive our wrist release – our wrists mustn't drive the clubhead.

And to many of us, this is the most puzzling thing. We don't understand how doing nothing can possibly increase clubhead speed so dramatically. Essentially, the increase in speed comes from the *change* in swing radius from tight to maximum during the wrist-unhinging process (between B and C in Figure 1). And again, some basic physics can explain this.

An object moving on a circular path travels faster when it's farther away from the centre of the circle. For example, imagine standing just one metre away from the North Pole. In one day, we'd travel one full circle, moving just six metres through space at a speed of only 25 *centimetres* per hour. If however, we stood farther away – on the equator – we'd still rotate one full circle in one day, but we'd travel around 40,000 kilometres through space at a speed of more than 1,600 *kilometres* per hour. Yet the earth rotates at the same speed. We may have experienced this effect during childhood when we rode on roundabouts. Sitting near the centre was easy, but if we moved towards the edge, we needed to hold on tightly to avoid being thrown off.

So our source of clubhead speed is keeping swing radius as *small* as possible, then making it as *large* as possible. Annex 1 describes the forces at work in the double pendulum, and the physics underlying the dramatic increase in speed.

## Basic instincts

A passive wrist release should be easy, because it's essentially the skill of doing nothing. But it's a bit of a problem, because we need to overcome some basic human instincts, which don't act in the best interests of our golf swings. After working relatively hard in the downswing to generate rotational speed and drive the first pendulum (our arms), we now need to leave the second pendulum (the club) alone (Figure 4). But in an activity where the aim is to hit a ball a long way with a weapon we hold in our hands, most of us find it difficult to do nothing with those hands. Our instincts, especially if we've played other striking sports, are to hit.

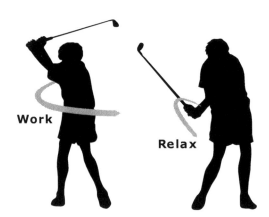

Figure 4. *The difficulty of the downswing: work – then relax*

In other striking sports like hockey and cricket, players position their hands slightly apart to apply leverage – a muscular, push-pull action of the hands and wrists – to the bat, to *force* rotation. In the golf swing though, we position our hands as *close* as possible (by overlapping our fingers) in order to *reduce* any tendency to lever the club.

Unnatural skills such as this exist in many sports. On steep slopes, the inexperienced downhill skier feels an urge to lean in towards the slope, seeking the security of solid ground, but they should lean out over the drop to keep an edge. The novice water-skier's instinct is to pull on the rope to stand up on their skis, but the boat needs to pull them up. The rock climber, at the point where fatigue and gravity are about to overcome ambition, wants to hug the rock, yet must stand away from it for maximum grip. But our instincts are wrong; physics has it right.

The skill of allowing a passive wrist release is actually that elusive swing quality, *good timing*. Many people perceive good timing as something we need to do – something we need to make happen at exactly the right time. But it isn't – a double pendulum has natural, perfect timing and our only task is to release it. Passively.

## Squaring the clubface

At this point, we can return to the need to square the clubface at impact. And it won't take long. We've already mentioned that clubface angle at impact is important, because it determines 85–95 per cent of initial ball flight direction. So why haven't we included it as a key skill in its own right? We haven't included it because it takes care of itself. It's part of the doing nothing skill – as long as we achieve a passive wrist release, double pendulum dynamics will return the clubhead square to the target line just as it reaches the ball. So we don't need to make any conscious effort to square the clubface. If we do, we'll simply interfere with the system's dynamics and the clubface will most likely *not* be square at impact. This again emphasises the importance of *allowing* the double pendulum to operate naturally, because it delivers both power and accuracy.

We've now covered the three elements of generating clubhead speed, so we might conclude by addressing a question dear to many of our hearts: can we occasionally 'go for a big one'?

## Going for a big one

We get immense satisfaction from hitting a huge, straight drive, especially in the presence of a crowd. But we're acutely embarrassed when we hook the ball wildly into the trees—especially in the presence of a crowd. Yet the two have a disturbingly close relationship: whenever an extra long drive appears in our brains, a wild hook tends to appear in our swings. We'll find out why by returning briefly to the three components of clubhead speed.

We've seen that we generate high clubhead speed if we (1) coordinate our muscular chains, (2) maintain a tight initial downswing radius, and (3) achieve a passive wrist release. Obviously, if we've developed good technique in (2) and (3), we can't improve on these – we should be doing them well all the time. So the only way we can generate higher clubhead speed is to *drive our muscular chains harder*. And it's difficult.

We can of course work harder, but the change in tempo tends to disrupt the precise coordination within the chain. The extra effort leaks out; it's wasted. Even if we do manage to create some extra rotational speed, the higher forces generated can cause the clubhead to escape from its tight radius too early. Again, the extra effort is wasted. And in our eagerness to work harder, we might be tempted to hit, which simply destroys everything. So while gaining extra distance is possible, the dangers far outweigh the small rewards. Put simply, we can only achieve extra distance by driving body rotation harder, *while keeping coordination, swing radius, and wrist release under the strictest control.*

For the sake of completeness, we should mention a few other techniques that can produce a little extra distance. These include using a longer club (within the rules), taking a longer backswing, shifting the swing hub forward during the downswing, and artificially delaying the wrist release beyond the passive release point (combined with a forced squaring of the clubface). Also, with modern drivers, teeing the ball higher and further forward – promoting a contact slightly 'on the up' – can be effective. Each can theoretically make a small difference, but they're mostly fraught with danger, because again, they change swing dynamics. Also, when the increase in clubhead speed is measured accurately, it never comes close to the additional speed theoretically available. Clearly, the extra effort leaks away. There seems little reason to introduce these high risks for such small rewards.

As a final – and important – note, if lack of distance is a problem, it almost certainly comes from deficiencies in key skills 3–5 (especially 4 and 5) – no amount of extra effort can compensate for poor technique. Going for a big one with faulty swing mechanics is always a terrible idea.

## TAKEAWAYS

*I* Natural forces within our arm-club lever system – a double pendulum – convert rotational speed into clubhead speed.

*I* We achieve maximum clubhead speed through a passive wrist release.

*I* Applying muscular force to the club with our hands and wrists will disrupt the system and *reduce* clubhead speed.

*I* A passive wrist release also produces a square clubface at impact.

*I* 'Going for a big one' is a bad idea.

# Part 4
## Making it happen

*Golfing cures can be divided into two main classes: there are the recognised conservative cures, and there are quack remedies. … [Quack] remedies do, in the long run, more harm than good. True, they give us a sort of spurious confidence for a short time; but, then, so would a whole-hearted belief that we would drive better if standing on our heads.*

—Bernard Darwin[31]

# 11

# Practice

To this point, we've been concerned with understanding the importance of swing thoughts and the key components of swing mechanics. This has been mainly theoretical, so now we need to put it into practice. Luckily, we know a lot about practice. We've a great deal of evidence gathered from many sports that we can use. This section is about maximising practice *effectiveness*.

## Ten thousand hours

At the 2012 London Olympic Games, Kimberly Rhodes (USA) won the skeet (shotgun) event, hitting 99 targets out of 100. For practice, Kimberly shoots up to 1,000 targets a day, seven days a week. She wears earplugs. She's hit more than *three million* targets in her career. It seems that repetition – practice – really *is* the cornerstone of mastering a skill. And it's easy to see why.

We know that automated golf swings reside in long-term memory and are beyond conscious control. Long-term memory doesn't deal in verbal logic, so no amount of conscious self-talk about keeping elbows in, or whatever, will have any beneficial effect. So once our swings achieve automaticity, we can *only* improve them through repetition; practice is now our only weapon. But how much practice do we need? And, what sort of practice is most effective?

Evidence collected from many sports and activities shows that achieving expert status requires at least 10,000 hours – around 10 years – of specific practice. This applies to cognitive and physical skills as diverse as musicianship, swimming, distance running, creative and scientific writing, mathematics, chess—even entrepreneurship.[32] Differences exist between activities. For example, expert musicians generally need more than 20 years of practice before they reach the top, usually achieving a performance peak in their mid-thirties. We might think of exceptions, but the figure of 10,000 hours holds up remarkably well under scientific scrutiny.

So, will simply hitting golf balls make us experts, as long as we do it for 10,000 hours? Well, almost, but not quite. We'll improve, but we won't necessarily become expert. The *type* of practice we undertake determines whether we achieve expert status or not. If our practice involves simply repeating the same swing – searching for technical perfection – we'll experience that most frustrating phenomenon – a *learning plateau*. Performers in all sports can experience the plateau effect; we tend to find our individual performance levels – our plateaus – and stay there. Good players in particular will recognise this – after months or years of improvement, they suddenly stagnate despite working on their swings as hard as ever.

When stuck on a plateau – and it's usually a stubborn barrier to progress – we might think we lack the talent to improve further.

But we'll see towards the end of this chapter that talent isn't a big influence in skill-dependent sports like golf. Stagnation comes from *inappropriate practice*. In other words, being stuck on a plateau is a sign we've progressed as far as we can through mere repetition.

Stagnation can come from practising fixed swing mechanics, because this constrains our joint movements. We effectively stifle the freedom of movement our joints require to exert fine control. A better strategy would be to practise golf shots. In other words, we need to venture outside our comfort zones by challenging our swings to produce shots that are currently beyond them. We need to attempt difficult shots, or produce shots under difficult circumstances. The technical term for such challenging practice is *deliberate practice*.[33] In golf, a better term might be *creative practice*, because we need to create difficult shot-making challenges. Creative practice is our route off the learning plateau.

## Creative practice

Severiano Ballesteros learnt his golf swing on beaches and in fields, using only a three-iron. Sheer necessity forced him to develop a swing that could produce any shot, under any circumstances, with just one (difficult) club. We might think Seve's learning conditions were poor, especially compared with today's sophisticated learning and practice facilities. But were they? Seve could produce better bunker shots using a three-iron than most of his fellow professionals could produce using any club of their choice, so his learning conditions can't have been that bad. In fact, these conditions may have been excellent, because Seve was constantly challenging his swing to produce good shots in difficult conditions. Without knowing it, Seve may have developed his wonderful swing through creative practice. It's doubtful he ever experienced a learning plateau.

Creative practice focuses on weaknesses. It asks our swings difficult questions. Can we vary each shot's trajectory, shape, and distance? Can we do this from different lies and slopes? And using different clubs? Can we do it in wind and rain? From rough and sand? With restricted backswings? Can we perform these shots when subjected to external distractions and pressure? When we undertake creative practice, we leave mindless repetition and playful engagement far behind. We indulge in 'repetition without repetition'.[34] We don't avoid things that make shots more difficult, such as bad weather. We do avoid things that make shots easier, for example, hitting all our shots from identical, flat, practice mat lies.

Creative practice is challenging, because we routinely fail. And failing can damage both our confidence and our egos. We can't (initially) produce the shots, so we feel and look like beginners again. Creative practice therefore demands high levels of commitment, effort, and concentration. But the rewards of focusing on shots rather than positions are considerable. First, it liberates us from the confusion and complexity of intricate golf swing mechanics. Second, our bodies have the freedom of movement they require to produce subtly different swings with equal precision. And third, we can minimise the influence of the artificial practice range environment, matching our shots more to the realities of the golf course.

In some sports and activities, performers view such difficult and challenging practice as sheer hard work – the opposite of fun. But in golf we're lucky, because we can create many shot-making challenges. We can exchange the stress of trying to achieve me-chanical perfection for the fun of hitting shots. In the words of one (ex-) coach, 'now, to finish the lesson, let's see who can hit the ball clean over the clubhouse …'

# Don't fiddle

For many of us, practice typically involves performing technical experiments. We continually adjust small technical details, hoping or believing they'll improve our swings. But will they? Interfering has the opposite effect, because even a small technical change will disrupt a well-automated swing routine. Unfortunately, in order to make *any* technical change, we need to focus consciously on our bodies and this will harm performance.

We may have already experienced this. When our swings mis-behave, we go to the range and start checking positions. This in-ternal focus de-automates our swings, so in addition to any (real or imagined) technical problem, we now have jerky, hesitant swings to deal with. The session deteriorates, as the more we try to fix the problem, the worse it gets. We enter a descending spiral of despair.

Something similar happens in darts. Darts players can suffer 'dartitis' – an inability to release the dart from their fingers prop-erly. It's a highly resistant problem, with some players suffering for years. The likely cause is that, in search of a cure, players abandon their external, target focus and replace it with an internal focus on their grip, arm action, or release action. Performance gets progressively worse, as players destroy the automaticity and free-dom of the natural throwing skill that previously served them so well.

So we have a dilemma. On the one hand, we need to think about *something* in relation to our swings, in order to improve them; on the other hand, we *mustn't* think about them because it tempts us to focus internally. Our main strategy must be to minimise the damage caused by internal focus. We can achieve this by treating the golf swing as a small number of big movement chunks (key skills 2–5) and developing each with external thoughts and analogies (discussed later, in Chapter 14). In this way, we can slowly massage the key components of errant swings back into shape.

## It's not my fault

Whenever we spot a swing position that deviates from perfect, we may – or may not – have discovered a fault. We may just have observed a natural part of our own swing signature – so a change in swing mechanics isn't necessary. We should consider many things before we change our golf swings, because the process of making permanent changes to automated swing routines is measured not in hours, weeks, or months, but in years. For most of us, it's normally better to practise *with* our swing, rather than continually *change* our swing.

But occasionally, changes may be unavoidable, for example through injury. Or a swing may have developed a serious technical flaw that clearly goes beyond individuality. We can certainly accomplish major technical changes, given (a lot of) time, through carefully designed practice and a good coach. But we mustn't underestimate how much damage we cause by interfering. Also, the list of outstanding players who have highly individual swings is simply endless – a well-practised 'fault' can be highly effective!

# Feedback

Blind squirrels can find nuts by accident. Equally, we can hit wonderful golf shots by accident – swing faults can cancel each other out. Similarly, we can hit poor shots despite getting most (but obviously not *all*) things right. So the shots we produce don't tell us everything about the quality of the swings that produced them. In fact, they can be misleading. In order to make rapid progress, we need better *feedback*.

It's difficult to overstate the importance of feedback – it's a major topic in its own right. We can't cover it all, but we should at least outline the essential points, because they can make a huge difference to practice effectiveness. Essentially, we need feedback because it's an essential component of implicit learning; without feedback, we can't learn. When we perform a golf swing, the shot we produce is our main feedback, but as we've said, it can be misleading. We need specific, relevant feedback about the clubhead path, wrist hinge angle and swing radius. And for maximum effectiveness, we need it after every swing.

Our main problem is that we only have 'feel' to rely on, because mostly, the club is out of sight. And unfortunately, feel rarely matches reality; whereas our swings may feel like Ernie Else's— they mostly aren't. Coaches – especially golf coaches – know the truth of the saying: 'feel is never real'. This is where technology comes into its own. Modern motion-capture equipment can record and analyse our swings in minute detail, so we can see all the important details immediately after each swing. We can then match the feel of swings with the reality of the pictures. In this way, we can develop the feels that produce technically better swings.

Ideally, we'd always have such equipment on hand, but it's expensive, so most of us don't. So, we need to rely on other, simpler sources of feedback. Unfortunately, there are few good substitutes. Some swing aids can give useful information about clubhead path, but there is no cheap, simple way to produce accurate feedback on wrist hinge angle or swing radius. We might buy a high-speed camera in the high street without taking out too large a mortgage, but better still, we can visit a coach who has some nice, expensive, kit.

The takeaway message is that practice with *accurate* and *relevant* feedback is more effective than practice in the dark, because it hurries along the implicit learning process.

## Do we need talent?

We mentioned earlier that talent isn't a big issue in golf. In fact, scientists debate whether talent exists at all.[35] But most of us believe in talent, so we should address the question: is lack of talent holding us back as golfers?

We might all agree that few of us could challenge Usain Bolt in a sprint race, however hard we train. He has natural, physical endowment – an innate ability, or inborn giftedness – that enables him to run faster than us. To excel at a power sport like sprinting, we'd need at least 85 per cent – preferably more than 90 per cent – of our leg muscle fibres to be of the fast twitch variety. Not slow twitch. And to excel at marathon running, we'd need the opposite.[36] No matter how hard we train, without an almost inhumanly high percentage of the right muscle fibres – endowed by some quirk of genetic inheritance – we stand no chance when we compete against the lucky, talented people who have them.

Talent is essentially genetic inheritance – in Usain Bolt's case, he inherited the right type of muscle fibres. In sports where success depends primarily on physical fitness – such as sprinting and marathon running – genetics explains around 50 per cent of the performance differences between individuals. In other words, genetic endowment is as important as *all the other influences combined*—including training.[37] So in any sport where speed, strength, power, or endurance is the prime requirement, talent clearly exists, in the guise of having inherited the right physiology. We need the right parents. Of course, even with the right genes, we still need to train. Our genes determine the size of the bucket; training determines how much we put in it.[38]

But golf is different. Swinging a golf club clearly depends more on *skill* than fitness. While a basic level of fitness helps, it isn't the prime requirement of making a good swing. So is talent a determining factor in skill-dependent sports such as golf? And exactly what is it? Can we measure it? The answers are surprising: no (probably), we don't know, and no. It's surprising, but in sports where fitness *isn't* the prime requirement, we can find no heritable differences between experts and everyone else. In high-skill activities, we don't have a muscle fibre equivalent. When we compare experts with beginners on any cognitive or physical characteristic related to skill, we can find no differences – beginners are just as likely to outperform the experts.

But we *can* find differences in many other things. In fact, we can explain the differences between experts and everyone else almost entirely by *non*genetic factors. These include abundant early play opportunities, early introduction to a wide range of sports, access to a good coach, regular practice, well-planned practice, strong parental support, and early exposure to playing with and against adults. The month we were born also has an effect, because older children in an age group have a size advantage. Bigger children tend to beat smaller children, irrespective of skill, so they become motivated, whereas the smaller children become dispirited and drop out.

Social factors can also be important in both fitness- and skill-dependent sports. Consider the dominance of Jamaican sprinters, Korean archers, and East African distance runners. Currently, we can't explain scientifically how these groups achieved – and now maintain – their dominance. Their superiority can't be explained genetically or by training, but *something* has caused it. Finnish javelin throwers are an interesting case. Finland has always pro-duced outstanding javelin throwers, but not discus, shot or ham-mer throwers. There's something going on in Finland that makes them good straight-line throwers – they even hold the world mo-bile phone throwing record, at 101 metres! It seems that once a group acquires a reputation for high achievement in a sport, 'things happen' to maintain the success. We currently can't ex-plain what these things are.

The important message for us is that we can relax about lacking talent, because in golf, there's probably nothing to lack. But we should be a little cautious – just because we can't measure differ-ences we shouldn't presume that differences don't exist. Science hasn't discovered everything about the human body and we obvi-ously can't measure things we don't know about. We should re-member: 'not everything measurable counts; not everything that counts is measurable'. We should also remember that high achievement in sport is never all genes or all training. It tends to be an optimum combination of the two – a complex *interaction* be-tween genetic endowment (nature) and specialised training condi-tions (nurture). It's the bucket plus its contents.

## Warm-up

To conclude this chapter, we'll consider warm-up, because it's a vital – and neglected – element of golf performance.[39] Our own personal experience tells us that without warm-up, our first few golf swings are sub-standard. Scientists have a name for this drop in performance: the *warm-up decrement*.

For any sport, warm-up is important, because it raises the temperature of our muscles, joints, ligaments, and tendons, enabling them to perform more efficiently. But warm-up in high-skill sports such as golf is important for another reason: without it, our automated swing routines won't fire properly. Even though we never forget a learned skill, it always takes some time to get it working properly. We know this, of course – we can't just walk from the car park to the first tee and strike the ball with any confidence. But why?

Our automated swing routines reside in long-term memory, but they don't actually *exist* there in any concrete form. We don't have a specific set of brain neurons devoted solely to performing our golf swings, lying dormant whenever we aren't swinging a golf club. What we have is a single, global, neural network, responsible for doing *everything*. The network is highly responsive and adaptable and constantly reconfigures itself to perform the next physical skill.

We can best understand how it works by considering the network to have a *focal point*, able to move around and relocate itself at any position. Each position represents the best place from where to send out a signal package that will trigger a particular movement skill. For two similar skills – for example, the golf swing and the baseball swing – the positions will be close together; the signal packages will overlap.

So the key to warming up our golf swings is to move the focal point from its current position – wherever that happens to be – to the golf swing position. To do this, we need to recalibrate our brains by performing the skill during warm-up. If we swim before we play golf, our focal points will have a long way to travel, because swimming skills aren't similar to golf swing skills. So we require a longer warm-up. This means we should be careful what we do – physically – before we play golf; even simple physical actions like playing a video game can significantly alter the position of the focal point.

The good news is that for most of us, just a few minutes warm-up can get our swings into reasonable shape. Better players however, need longer, because they have smaller margins of error and need to locate their focal points more precisely. Professional tennis players, baseball players, and golfers routinely hit balls for up to an hour before competing. It's also wise to leave only a short time gap between warm-up and play – and to make the last few shots on the range the same as the first tee shot.

## Takeaways

𝟙 Varied, challenging (creative) practice develops adaptable, self-correcting golf swings.

𝟙 Making permanent changes to swing mechanics is a lengthy process, because it disrupts automaticity.

𝟙 Practice with accurate and relevant feedback is more effective than practice without feedback.

𝟙 Talent isn't a proven concept in skill-dependent sports.

𝟙 Pre-session warm-up is essential in high-skill sports, especially for better players.

# 12

# Little swings

So NOW WE KNOW HOW TO DEVELOP SWINGS that will produce long, straight shots, and we find ourselves close to the green. Our next challenge is to perform a series of swings that are fundamentally different from the full golf swing: the pitch, chip, and putt. We have more research on these little swings than on the full swing, mostly investigating mental focus. We needn't rehearse mental focus again here (except, briefly, for putting), but we'll consider little swing mechanics, because they're different—and can cause considerable frustration and anguish.

## The pitch

The pitch is a shot that requires a less-than-full swing, but still involves a wrist hinge. In skill-learning terminology, it's closer to a fine motor skill than a gross motor skill. Gross motor skills are big movements, involving the whole body: the torso, larger limbs, and larger muscle groups. The movements are relatively crude and imprecise – the full golf swing is a perfect example. In contrast, fine motor skills require greater precision and we perform them with smaller muscles, which can apply fine control. Threading a needle is a good example. The pitch falls somewhere between these two extremes.

In theory, it would make most sense to control the pitch with the smaller, more accurate muscles of our hands and wrists. However, we can't, because hinging our wrists invokes double pendulum dynamics, which demand *passive* hands and wrists. So the pitch needs to be a normal double pendulum swing, controlled primarily by our large and clumsy trunk and shoulder muscles – just a miniature version. But unfortunately, a miniature double pendulum swing is far from normal. Things change.

First, double pendulums are all about generating clubhead speed – maximising distance – but in the pitch swing we're more concerned with distance *control*. So the powerful double pendulum action – such a huge benefit in the full swing – is now a bit of a liability. Second, whenever we make a less-than-full swing, we create a different starting orientation for the double pendulum. Because we don't swing back so far and/or hinge our wrists less, we create different starting positions for both pendulums and the angle between them. And unfortunately, this alters the double pendulum's natural dynamics.

We haven't mentioned this previously, but double pendulums are highly sensitive to the starting positions of their components. Essentially, for every combination of pendulum positions and hinge angle, there's a slightly different natural pendulum action. It still works well, but the dynamics are different. Essentially, every pitch swing requires a unique combination of swing length, swing speed and wrist hinge angle, and each modification changes the swing's dynamics and – most importantly – its feel. To see exactly how the pendulum dynamics change, we can find interactive double pendulum models on various websites (see note 29, for an example). By choosing different starting orientations, we can see how the downswing action changes. So what can we do to overcome these changes and develop good pitching swings?

First, we can make a full swing whenever possible, as this invokes normal double pendulum dynamics, which should be familiar. For example, a slightly slower swing, or a slightly open clubface might just enable us to make a full swing. Gripping down the club will do the same, but it shortens the second pendulum, which again changes the dynamics. We might restrict the number of changes we make, for example, achieving a consistent wrist hinge angle or backswing length, just varying one of them. But this isn't an exact science – the only sure way to develop good pitching swings is to practise them at least as much as the full swing. And before each pitch, we should take as many practice swings as we can get away with.

## The chip

The chip is essentially a short pitch, where the distance to the target is short enough to dispense with the wrist hinge – if we so wish. And it's an even better example of a fine motor skill performed with the wrong muscles. Trial and error has found that a stiff-wristed technique – at least during the downswing – is most effective for the chip. Although this technique uses our large shoulder muscles, it's still more effective than using hand and wrist muscles. The reason it's more effective is because it takes

95

double pendulum dynamics out of the equation – the wrist hinge doesn't operate.

The stiff-wristed downswing is effectively a simple, *single* pendulum action that's easier to control; we overcome the problems of altered double pendulum dynamics. We'd do the same for the pitch, if only we could generate enough single pendulum power. Many coaches recommend a stiff-wristed putting action for the chip, for both the backswing and downswing. This has the same beneficial effect: it invokes simple, single pendulum dynamics.

## The putt

We're concerned here with the best way to swing a putter, not how to read a green, choose a line, or aim. Similar to chipping, a stiff-wristed putting technique has been found to be effective. And, again, this makes sense as it invokes single pendulum dynamics and makes the swing simpler to perform. We again remove the problem of altered double pendulum dynamics. So why do things go so wrong, so often, in such a simple movement? Partly, it's because we're using the wrong muscles, but there's a more important reason: we're yet again hooked on mechanics.

When our putting swings misbehave, most of us – just as in the full swing – instinctively look for a mechanical 'fault'. But as we now know, the cause of all bad swings lies upstream, in our brains. This also applies to the pitch and the chip swings, but we'll rehearse it again here because it's on the putting green where an inappropriate mental focus can wreak most havoc with our swings, and – especially – our scores.

We have clear evidence that adopting an external mental focus is a critical – probably *the* critical – element in putting. Our task in developing an effective putting swing is therefore to adjust our errant mental focus, rather than our simple swing mechanics. Just as in the full swing, an internal focus constrains our putting swings into inflexible, mechanical actions, unable to adapt and self-correct. They lack the subtle freedom of movement required to achieve precise putterhead control. In contrast, an external focus frees up our joints, enabling them to adjust the putterhead path continually in order to achieve the desired result. Watching good putters is like watching good drivers of a golf ball: they both have fluid, effortless, unconstrained swings. Good putting strokes tend to look more like graceful clouds than jerky clocks.

So we might venture a few thoughts on external foci we can use in putting. We have quite a choice. We can focus on the line of the putt, the hole, the aiming point, the putterhead path, or a movie of the ball travelling along the line and into the hole. The aiming line on the ball is also useful: we can focus on the ball rolling without a wobbling line. It's interesting to note that performance in all golf swings improves as the external focus moves farther away from our bodies. So focusing on the hole should work better than focusing on the ball or putterhead. Also, our brains tend to consider the club as part of the body – because it's attached – so focusing somewhere beyond the clubhead should work best. Some personal experimentation is required.

The essential point is that mental focus in putting is more important than putting swing mechanics. Although it's wise to pay some attention to establishing a mechanically sound putting action, it's a bad idea to fixate on it. It's actually surprising that we pay so much attention to putting mechanics, because they're not complicated: there's no muscular chain, no change in swing radius, no double pendulum, and no wrist release. In such a simple action, it makes little sense to *introduce* complications, such as using a radically different putter, grip, or stance. These are just additional and unnecessary variables to manage, making the putting stroke more high maintenance.

Finally, we can consider briefly one other important influence on putting – how much time we take over the putt. We're referring here to time taken over making the putting stroke, not time spent reading the putt. In everyone except complete beginners, taking more time over a putt harms performance, because it increases the likelihood of adopting an internal focus. So the Nike motto again takes the day. Coaches advise players to 'putt like you did when you were a child. Look—then putt'. In scientific terms, this is excellent advice.

## Takeaways

*I* Less-than-full (pitching) swings invoke modified double pendulum dynamics, which change the swing's feel.

*I* A stiff-wristed, single pendulum action is most effective for chipping and putting, because it invokes single pendulum dynamics.

*I* An external focus is the key element in an effective putting swing.

*I* Except for beginners, taking extra time over the putting stroke harms performance.

# 13

# Coaching

EVERYTHING DISCUSSED SO FAR is as relevant to teaching as it is to learning, but a few issues may be particularly important for the coach. This section addresses only the general principles of coaching sports skills; specific golf coaching techniques must remain the domain of the teaching professional.

## Images and analogies

An external mental focus, as we've seen, helps us learn and develop our golf swings. And the same applies to the instructions given by a coach – externally focused instructions are more effective than internally focused instructions. Coaches need to translate technical requirements into a language the pupil's brain can compute: simple, external thoughts or analogies. And we shouldn't underestimate the effects of a coach encouraging an external, compared to an internal focus. We have evidence that giving internally focused instructions has no better effect than giving no instructions at all—simple trial and error gets us there just as quickly. And – depressingly – internally focused instructions can actually have a *worse* effect than giving no instructions at all. This suggests that simple, implicit learning can be more effective than well-intentioned, but inappropriate coaching.

Similarly, after each swing, the nature of the feedback given is equally important. Feedback referring to an external image or analogy is more effective than feedback referring internally to body parts and positions. And most importantly, players – especially beginners – tend to *prefer* an external focus. They say it feels more natural to focus on the clubhead, the ball, or an analogy, rather than body parts. Only a brave coach ignores a teaching strategy that's both more effective and more acceptable to pupils.

## Making good players better

Good players, already swinging effectively, present the coach with a tricky problem: how to make good swings even better. One strategy is to look for technical deviations from 'perfect' and fix them. The alternative approach is to challenge the player to use their current swing to explore and extend their shot-making boundaries. In other words, the coach can introduce the player to creative practice.

This is an important issue for coaches, because it suggests a re-think of what constitutes effective coaching. Adjusting swing mechanics is straightforward (and what the player expects), but it may not be in the player's best interests. It's entirely possible that coaching methods focusing on body parts, angles and movements will improve players' technical knowledge and give them text-book swings—but maybe not more effective swings.

# The player-coach

Many top players write coaching books. Top players clearly have highly effective golf swings, but it isn't exactly clear whether this makes them good coaches. Top players have a unique problem: a powerful mental block about their swing mechanics.

If we ask a beginner to describe their last swing, they'll give a detailed and accurate description – they can recall everything, because they consciously attend to technical details while they swing. Coaches have a phrase: 'scratch a beginner and you'll find a coach', referring to their unique recall ability. But if we ask a good player the same question, we'll receive a shorter answer—because they don't *know* what they did. Top players just step up to the ball and release their well-automated swing routines; they just swing. So when asked about a good shot that maybe won a championship, a top player will simply thank God, their coach or their caddie, because they don't actually know what they did. We call this phenomenon *expertise-induced amnesia*[40] – a common trait in skilful people.

However, good players are extremely knowledgeable about general golf swing technique – ingrained by hours of practice and coaching – so they can describe accurately all the positions and moves that make up *the* golf swing. Their coaching books may therefore be technically excellent—but not necessarily based on their own swings.

## TAKEAWAYS

𝟙  Externally focused instructions are more effective than internally focused instructions.

𝟙  Externally focused feedback is more effective than internally focused feedback.

𝟙  Technical changes to the swing have to be 'coded' into simple thoughts and images, acceptable to the pupil's brain.

𝟙  Developing good players' shot-making capabilities is a better coaching strategy than adjusting their swings towards 'perfect'.

# 14

# After ecstasy, the laundry

THIS ZEN SAYING reminds us there's work to do. After the ecstasy of discovering the golf swing isn't as complicated as we thought, we now have the laundry of having to *do* something. So we need some practical ways to improve the five key skills. The essential quality of any new approach to play or practice must be *simplicity*. Only when our brains are dealing with simple concepts can we be sure that our memories are operating appropriately. Our essential requirements are some practice aids, some swing mantras and a few songs. First, the practice aids.

## Practice aids

For our next visit to the range, we might take with us a cardboard box, a large wheel, a corkscrew, a blanket, and a flail. The cardboard box we actually have to take with us, the rest can be images in our minds. They're all external foci that will help develop the key physical skills.

### The cardboard box

Place the box parallel to the target line just outside the toe of the club at address. If the box doesn't move at impact, the swing path was fine. Focusing on the ball and being aware of the box – and moving one but not the other – is an excellent external focus to encourage an accurate swing path. If attention wanders, replace the cardboard box with a concrete block.

### The large wheel

The perimeter of a large (imaginary) wheel can represent an approximate path for the clubhead to follow. The section we're most interested in is from the ball to somewhere behind our shoulders. We concluded earlier that the concept of a two-dimensional plane (like a wheel) is inappropriate for understanding the golf swing, but this doesn't stop us using it as a swing aid – it can represent a path through our swing corridor. Swinging the clubhead somewhere close to the edge of the wheel makes our task of self-correcting – rounding it up – easier.

### The corkscrew

We can view our downswing body rotation as the action of screwing a corkscrew into the ground, starting with our feet, then our hips, then our shoulders. It's important to think of the corkscrew, not our feet, hips, or shoulders. This will develop coordination within our muscular chains.

### The blanket

We can imagine the club is a blanket. As we start the downswing, we feel we're wrapping the blanket closely around our bodies. This will encourage a tight initial downswing radius.

### The flail

A flail – two sticks joined by a hinge – is a medieval tool used for threshing grain; it's a double pendulum. Farm workers discovered that two hinged sticks delivered more threshing power than a single stick. We can imagine threshing the ball, not thrashing it. This will encourage a passive wrist release.

Next, we need something to chant.

## Swing mantras

Chanting a simple mantra (preferably with good golf swing rhythm) can promote two or more skills. With some imagination, it may be possible to promote three – or even all four – but most of us will find this too difficult. The table below contains some simple thoughts that will generate signal packages promoting combinations of key skills.

| Thought | Key skills |
|---|---|
| *'Flail past the box'* | Passive wrist release<br>Accurate clubhead path |
| *'Keep it tight – let it fly'*<br>(clubhead) | Tight radius<br>Passive wrist release |
| *'Wrap and release'*<br>(blanket and clubhead) | Tight radius<br>Passive wrist release |
| *'Screw and sling'*<br>(corkscrew and clubhead) | Muscular chain<br>Passive wrist release |

What we really need is a mantra to include all four physical skills:

*'Screw, wrap, and flail past the box'*

But it's too complicated – four separate thoughts in two tenths of a second can't happen. Unfortunately, no single image or mantra can embody all four physical skills. Except one—the golf swing! And this isn't as farfetched as we might imagine. In sport, watching good performers is a proven way to absorb complex skills. The scientific term for this is *vicarious practice*. So we could actually have a single swing thought for all four skills:

*'Ernie Else'*

Finally, we need some songs to sing.

## Swing songs

Singing songs (quietly) is a proven way of avoiding an internal focus, especially under pressure. Again, it helps if the song has good golf swing rhythm and if the imagery relates to a desired swing quality. Songs about long, winding roads, or about taking it easy, might be particularly appropriate. And if we choose the song about hitting with rhythm sticks, we should focus on the rhythm stick—not the hitting.

These simple thoughts and images are far-removed from today's high-tech golf swing – but we thrive on such simplicity.

# 15

# Final thought

THIS SCIENTIFIC ANALYSIS suggests there's a simpler, yet more effective way to learn and develop the golf swing than submerging ourselves in technical complexity. It's strange that the power of modern science has simply told us that we've made the golf swing too scientific. This isn't to say that golf swing science is of no use—quite the opposite. Scientific scrutiny of the swing is hugely valuable and we can learn much from it – our only problem is using it directly for learning and teaching.

Overall, this analysis sends us three clear messages.

First, somewhere along the line, the way we learn and teach the golf swing lost its way. Exactly when it happened isn't clear, but it was probably sometime around the invention of the high-speed camera.

Second, we would learn and develop the golf swing more rapidly by returning – part way, at least – to the old-school method of focusing on simple images and feels to promote fewer, more global swing qualities. Swing coaches of previous eras, like Ernest Jones, certainly knew a thing or two about effective learning and teaching—even if they didn't know the scientific basis of *why* their methods worked so well.

Third, the analysis provides support for some long-standing golf swing fundamentals, such as lagging the clubhead. It's clear that we know a great deal about how to swing a golf club – it's just that we've smothered it in mostly irrelevant detail.

As a concluding note, we should recognise that leaving behind all the theories, opinions, and complexities will be difficult, because they fascinate us. We'll always be attracted to space age, high-tech approaches to problem solving and we'll no doubt continue to apply this sort of thinking to the golf swing. In the words of psychologist Abraham Maslow: 'When you first get a good hammer, every problem looks like a nail'. And it's always been like this. More than 100 years ago, Bernard Darwin noted exactly the same problem:

> *When once the bacillus of what I may call theoretic practising has attacked us, he is terribly difficult to get rid of … we may have worried ourselves sick with theories, so that we know ourselves to be fools, and yet we won't stop; we will play out to the bitter end our tragedy ….*

—Bernard Darwin[41]

# Annex 1
# The science

## Acceleration

For straight-line motion, an object's acceleration depends on the force acting on it and it's mass. These are related by the formula:

$$force = mass \cdot acceleration$$

Or, because we're most interested in acceleration, we can rearrange the formula:

$$acceleration = \frac{force}{mass}$$

However, the golf swing is a rotational movement, so we need an equivalent formula for rotation. The rotational equivalent of force is torque, the equivalent of mass is moment of inertia (MOI), and the equivalent of linear acceleration is angular acceleration. These are related by the formula:

$$torque = MOI \cdot angular\ acceleration$$

We're most interested in angular acceleration, because this is associated with clubhead speed, so again, we can rearrange the formula:

$$angular\ acceleration = \frac{torque}{MOI}$$

We can therefore increase angular acceleration in two ways:

- ⚡ Increase torque
- ⚡ Reduce MOI.

To increase torque, we need to drive body rotation harder. To reduce MOI, we need to consider the formula linking it with the mass of our arms plus club and swing radius:

$$MOI = mass.\,radius^2$$

So to reduce MOI, we can do one of two things:

- ⚡ Reduce the mass of our arms and club
- ⚡ Reduce the swing radius.

We can't reduce the mass of our arms or club, so the only thing we can do is reduce the swing radius. Note that MOI varies with r *squared,* so reducing swing radius has a huge effect on MOI.

## Forces in the double pendulum

All objects obey the laws of motion – when they move, they do so predictably. So 'an object will remain at rest or move with a constant velocity in a straight line unless it is acted upon by forces' (Newton's first law of motion). During the downswing, the clubhead follows a curved path, so obviously a force is acting on it. That force is the tension in our arms and the club shaft, pulling the clubhead towards the centre of rotation. We call this a *centripetal* (centre seeking) force.[42]

It's the same in hammer throwing – the tendency of the ball is to fly away in a straight line, but the tension in the thrower's arms and the wire apply a centripetal force that pulls it onto a circular path. When the thrower lets go, the centripetal force is removed and the hammer flies away in a straight line (Figure 5).

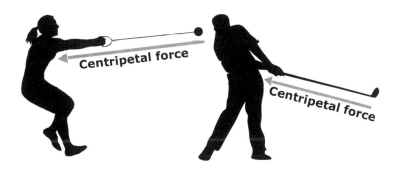

Figure 5. *Centripetal force: hammer throw and golf swing*

In the golf downswing, the clubhead's tendency is also to move in a straight line – it wants to fly away from our bodies. But because we hold our wrist hinge, we apply a centripetal force and it moves in an arc. As swing speed increases, we reach a critical point where the outward-acting forces generated by the swing exceed the centripetal force applied by our wrists. At this point, our wrists unhinge and the clubhead starts to fly rapidly outwards. It still follows a curved path, but with an increasing radius, reaching a maximum at the fully straightened-out impact position. The massive increase in clubhead speed during this process comes from the change in swing radius, from an initially tight configuration to the final maximum position. Some basic physics can explain this.

Whenever an object (the clubhead) moves on a circular path, it has two types of velocity. First, it has angular velocity: how many degrees of the circle the clubhead moves through in a given time. Second, it has linear velocity: the speed with which it moves through space. In the golf swing, we want to maximise the club-head's linear velocity, because this is clubhead speed. Linear velocity, angular velocity, and radius of rotation are related by the formula:

$$linear\ velocity = angular\ velocity\,.\,radius$$

So to increase clubhead speed we can do two things:

- Increase angular velocity
  and/or
- Increase radius of rotation.

We generate high angular velocity by powering our muscular chains and keeping swing radius small. Now, we need to create a large swing radius by unhinging our wrists and allowing the clubhead to fly away.

# Annex 2
# Bibliography

THE REFERENCE LIST BELOW contains the main scientific articles used in writing this book. Abstracts of most articles can be downloaded free of charge from academic databases, such as *Pub Med*: http://www.ncbi.nlm.nih.gov/pubmed/. Full articles can sometimes be downloaded free of charge, however most require either a journal subscription or an individual purchase. Free abstracts and a larger selection of articles can be obtained from *Google Scholar*: http://scholar.google.com/. Copyright restrictions prevent the author from supplying copies of articles.

### *Memory*

1. Kihlstrom, J. F., J. Dorfman, et al. (2007). Implicit and explicit memory and learning. The Blackwell companion to consciousness. I. M. Velmans and S. Schneider. Oxford Blackwell: 525-539.
2. Miller, G. A. (1956). The magical number seven, plus or minus two: some limits on our capacity for processing information. Psychological review 63(2): 81.

### *Skill*

3. Abernethy, B. (1991). Acquisition of motor skills. Better coaching, advanced coach's manual. Improving the athlete. Australian Coaching Council, Canberra 6: 69-98.
4. Ajemian, R., A. D'Ausilio, et al. (2010). Why professional athletes need a prolonged period of warm-up and other peculiarities of human motor learning. J Mot Behav 42(6): 381-388.
5. Bezzola, L., S. Mérillat, et al. (2011). Training-induced neural plastic-

ity in golf novices. The Journal of neuroscience 31(35): 12444-12448.

6.   Boutin, A. and Y. Blandin (2010). Cognitive underpinnings of con-
     textual interference during motor learning. Acta psychologica
     135(2): 233-239.

7.   Boutin, A. and Y. Blandin (2010). On the cognitive processes under-
     lying contextual interference: Contributions of practice schedule,
     task similarity and amount of practice. Human movement science
     29(6): 910-920.

8.   Button, C. and G. Pepping (2002). Enhancing Skill Acquisition in
     Golf–Some Key Principles. Internet article: http://www. coachesinfo.
     com/category/golf.

9.   Floyer-Lea, A. and P. Matthews (2004). Changing brain networks
     for visuomotor control with increased movement automaticity.
     Journal of neurophysiology 92(4): 2405-2412.

10.  Gorman, A. (2008). Skill Automaticity in Sport: Coaching Strategies
     to Minimise'Paralysis by Analysis'.

11.  Hardy, L., R. Mullen, et al. (1996). Knowledge and conscious control
     of motor actions under stress. British Journal of Psychology 87(4):
     621-636.

12.  Hernandez, A. E., A. Mattarella-Micke, et al. (2011). Age of Acquisi-
     tion in Sport: Starting Early Matters. The American journal of psy-
     chology 124(3): 253-260.

13.  Mazzoni, P. and N. S. Wexler (2009). Parallel explicit and implicit
     control of reaching. PloS one 4(10): e7557.

14.  McLeod, P., N. Reed, et al. (2003). How fielders arrive in time to
     catch the ball. Nature 426(20): 224.

15.  Milton, J. (2010). Leading Article: Discovering Golf's Innermost
     Truths: A New Approach to Teaching the Game. International Jour-
     nal of Sports Science and Coaching 5(-1): 115-118.

16.  Mullen, R., L. Hardy, et al. (2007). Implicit and explicit control of
     motor actions: Revisiting some early evidence. British Journal of
     Psychology 98(1): 141-156.

17.  Poldrack, R. A., F. W. Sabb, et al. (2005). The neural correlates of

motor skill automaticity. The Journal of neuroscience 25(22): 5356-5364.

18.  Porter, J. M. and R. A. Magill (2010). Systematically increasing contextual interference is beneficial for learning sport skills. Journal of sports sciences 28(12): 1277-1285.

19.  Reber, A. S. (1992). An evolutionary context for the cognitive unconscious [1]. Philosophical Psychology 5(1): 33-51.

20.  Reed, N., P. McLeod, et al. (2010). Implicit knowledge and motor skill: What people who know how to catch don't know. Consciousness and cognition 19(1): 63-76.

21.  Steenbergen, B., J. van der Kamp, et al. (2010). Implicit and explicit learning: applications from basic research to sports for individuals with impaired movement dynamics. Disability & Rehabilitation 32(18): 1509-1516.

22.  Wulf, G., N. McNevin, et al. (2001). The automaticity of complex motor skill learning as a function of attentional focus. The Quarterly Journal of Experimental Psychology: Section A 54(4): 1143-1154.

23.  Wulf, G., C. Shea, et al. (2010). Motor skill learning and performance: a review of influential factors. Medical education 44(1): 75-84.

## *Focus of attention*

24.  Beilock, S. L., B. I. Bertenthal, et al. (2004). Haste does not always make waste: Expertise, direction of attention, and speed versus accuracy in performing sensorimotor skills. Psychonomic Bulletin & Review 11(2): 373-379.

25.  Beilock, S. L. and S. Gonso (2008). Putting in the mind versus putting on the green: Expertise, performance time, and the linking of imagery and action. The Quarterly Journal of Experimental Psychology 61(6): 920-932.

26.  Beilock, S. L., W. A. Jellison, et al. (2006). On the causal mechanisms of stereotype threat: Can skills that don't rely heavily on working memory still be threatened? Personality and Social Psychology Bulletin 32(8): 1059-1071.

27. Chauvel, G., F. Maquestiaux, et al. (2012). Age effects shrink when motor learning is predominantly supported by nondeclarative, automatic memory processes: Evidence from golf putting. The Quarterly Journal of Experimental Psychology 65(1): 25-38.

28. DeCaro, M. S. and S. L. Beilock (2010). The benefits and perils of attentional control. Effortless Attention. M. Csikszentmihalyi and B. Bruya. Effortless Attention: A New Perspective in the Cognitive Science of Attention and Action., MIT Press: 51-73.

29. Ford, P., N. J. Hodges, et al. (2009). An evaluation of end-point trajectory planning during skilled kicking. Motor Control.

30. Hossner, E. J. and F. Ehrlenspiel (2010). Time-referenced effects of an internal vs. external focus of attention on muscular activity and compensatory variability. Frontiers in Psychology 1.

31. Lam, W., J. Maxwell, et al. (2010). Probing the allocation of attention in implicit (motor) learning. Journal of sports sciences 28(14): 1543-1554.

32. Lam, W. K., R. S. W. Masters, et al. (2010). Cognitive demands of error processing associated with preparation and execution of a motor skill. Consciousness and cognition 19(4): 1058-1061.

33. Lawrence, G. P., V. M. Gottwald, et al. (2011). Internal and external focus of attention in a novice form sport. Research quarterly for exercise and sport 82(3): 431-441.

34. Lewthwaite, R. and G. Wulf (2010). Grand challenge for movement science and sport psychology: embracing the social-cognitive–affective–motor nature of motor behavior. Frontiers in Psychology 1.

35. Marchant, D., M. Greig, et al. (2006). Attentional focusing strategies influence muscle activity during isokinetic bicep curls. Athletic Insight. Online journal.

36. Marchant, D. C. (2010). Attentional focusing instructions and force production. Frontiers in Psychology 1.

37. Marchant, D. C., M. Greig, et al. (2011). Instructions to adopt an external focus enhance muscular endurance. Research quarterly for

exercise and sport 82(3): 466-473.

38. Marteniuk, R. G. and C. P. Bertram (2009). Selective Attention in Golf: Managing the Keys to the Door. International Journal of Sports Science and Coaching 4: 247-253.

39. Masters, R. and J. Burns (1995). Mind Swings: The Thinking Way to Better Golf, Aurum Press.

40. McNevin, N. H., C. H. Shea, et al. (2003). Increasing the distance of an external focus of attention enhances learning. Psychological Research 67(1): 22-29.

41. Peh, S. Y. C., J. Y. Chow, et al. (2011). Focus of attention and its impact on movement behaviour. Journal of science and medicine in sport 14(1): 70-78.

42. Perkins-Ceccato, N., R. P. Steve, et al. (2003). Effects of focus of attention depend on golfers' skill. Journal of sports sciences 21(8): 593-600.

43. Poolton, J., J. Maxwell, et al. (2006). Benefits of an external focus of attention: Common coding or conscious processing? Journal of sports sciences 24(1): 89-99.

44. Porter, J. M., E. J. Ostrowski, et al. (2010). Standing long-jump performance is enhanced when using an external focus of attention. The Journal of Strength & Conditioning Research 24(7): 1746.

45. Schücker, L., N. Hagemann, et al. (2009). The effect of attentional focus on running economy. Journal of sports sciences 27(12): 1241-1248.

46. Toner, J. and A. Moran (2011). The effects of conscious processing on golf putting proficiency and kinematics. Journal of sports sciences 29(7): 673-683.

47. Uehara, L. A., C. Button, et al. (2008). The effects of focus of attention instructions on novices learning soccer chip. Brazilian Journal of Biomotricity(002): 63-77.

48. van Lier, W. H., J. van der Kamp, et al. (2011). Perception and action in golf putting: Skill differences reflect calibration. Journal of Sport and Exercise Psychology 33(3): 349.

49. Weiss, S. M. (2011). The Effects of Reinvestment of Conscious Processing on Switching Focus of Attention. Research quarterly for exercise and sport 82(1): 28-36.

50. Wulf, G. (2007). Attentional focus and motor learning: A review of 10 years of research. Bewegung und Training 1: 4-14.

51. Wulf, G., S. Chiviacowsky, et al. (2010). Frequent external-focus feedback enhances motor learning. Frontiers in Psychology 1.

52. Wulf, G., J. S. Dufek, et al. (2010). Increased jump height and reduced EMG activity with an external focus. Human movement science 29(3): 440-448.

53. Wulf, G., B. Lauterbach, et al. (1999). The learning advantages of an external focus of attention in golf. Research quarterly for exercise and sport 70: 120-126.

54. Wulf, G., N. McConnel, et al. (2002). Enhancing the learning of sport skills through external-focus feedback. Journal of Motor Behavior 34(2): 171-182.

55. Wulf, G. and C. H. Shea (2002). Principles derived from the study of simple skills do not generalize to complex skill learning. Psychonomic Bulletin & Review 9(2): 185-211.

56. Wulf, G. and J. Su (2007). An external focus of attention enhances golf shot accuracy in beginners and experts. Research quarterly for exercise and sport 78(4): 384.

57. Zhu, F., J. Poolton, et al. (2011). Neural co-activation as a yardstick of implicit motor learning and the propensity for conscious control of movement. Biological Psychology.

58. Zhu, F. F., J. M. Poolton, et al. (2011). Implicit motor learning promotes neural efficiency during laparoscopy. Surgical endoscopy: 1-6.

## *Performing under pressure*

59. Beilock, S. L. and T. H. Carr (2001). On the fragility of skilled performance: What governs choking under pressure? Journal of experimental psychology: General 130(4): 701.

60. Beilock, S. L. and R. Gray (2007). Why do athletes choke under pressure? Handbook of sport psychology: 425-444.

61. Cooke, A., M. Kavussanu, et al. (2011). Effects of competitive pressure on expert performance: Underlying psychological, physiological, and kinematic mechanisms. Psychophysiology 48(8): 1146-1156.

62. DeCaro, M. S., R. D. Thomas, et al. (2011). Choking under pressure: Multiple routes to skill failure. Journal of experimental psychology: General 140(3): 390.

63. Lam, W. K., J. P. Maxwell, et al. (2009). Analogy learning and the performance of motor skills under pressure. Journal of sport & exercise psychology 31(3): 337.

64. Masters, R. S. W. (1992). Knowledge, knerves and know-how: The role of explicit versus implicit knowledge in the breakdown of a complex motor skill under pressure. British Journal of Psychology 83(3): 343-358.

65. O'Callaghan, T. (2011). Sian Beilock: why we screw up when the heat is on. The New Scientist 211(2820): 28-29.

66. Otten, M. P. (2007). Choking vs. clutch performance: A study of sport performance under pressure, ProQuest.

67. Oudejans, R. R. D., W. Kuijpers, et al. (2011). Thoughts and attention of athletes under pressure: skill-focus or performance worries? Anxiety, Stress, & Coping 24(1): 59-73.

### *Dynamic systems*

68. Davids, K. and J. Baker (2007). Genes, environment and sport performance: Why the Nature-Nurture dualism is no longer relevant. Sports Medicine 37(11): 961-980.

69. Davids, K., C. Button, et al. (2008). Dynamics of skill acquisition: A constraints-led approach, Human Kinetics Publishers.

70. Davids, K. and P. Glazier (2010). Deconstructing neurobiological coordination: the role of the biomechanics-motor control nexus. Exercise and sport sciences reviews 38(2): 86.

71. Glazier, P. (2011). Movement Variability in the Golf Swing: Theo-

retical, Methodological, and Practical Issues. Research quarterly for exercise and sport 82(2): 157-161.

72. Glazier, P. and K. Davids (2005). Is there such a thing as a 'perfect' golf swing. International Society of Biomechanics in Sports' Coaches Information Service.

73. Glazier, P. S. (2010). Augmenting golf practice through the manipulation of physical and informational constraints, Taylor & Francis.

74. Glazier, P. S. (2010). Game, set and match? Substantive issues and future directions in performance analysis. Sports Medicine 40(8): 625-634.

75. Glazier, P. S. and K. Davids (2009). On analysing and interpreting variability in motor output. Journal of science and medicine in sport 12(4): e2-e3.

76. Jenkins, S. (2008). Dynamics of Skill Acquisition: A Constraints-Led Approach. International Journal of Sports Science and Coaching 3(1): 147-151.

77. Langdown, B. L., M. Bridge, et al. (2012). Movement variability in the golf swing.

## *Swing mechanics*

78. Arnold, D. N. (2010). The Science of a Drive. Notices of the AMS 57(4).

79. Ball, K. and R. Best (2007). Different centre of pressure patterns within the golf stroke I: Cluster analysis. Journal of sports sciences 25(7): 757-770.

80. Ball, K. A. and R. Best (2011). Golf styles and centre of pressure patterns when using different golf clubs. Journal of sports sciences 29(6): 587-590.

81. Betzler, N., S. Monk, et al. (2008). From the double pendulum model to full-body simulation: evolution of golf swing modeling. Sports Technology 1(4-5): 175-188.

82. Brown, S. J., A. M. Nevill, et al. (2011). Determination of the swing technique characteristics and performance outcome relationship in

golf driving for low handicap female golfers. J Sports Sci 29(14): 1483-1491.

83. Burden, A. M., P. N. Grimshaw, et al. (1998). Hip and shoulder rotations during the golf swing of sub-10 handicap players. Journal of sports sciences 16(2): 165-176.

84. Cheetham, P. J., P. E. Martin, et al. (2001). The importance of stretching the'X-Factor'in the downswing of golf: the'X-Factor stretch'. Optimising performance in golf: 192-199.

85. Chu, Y., T. C. Sell, et al. (2010). The relationship between biomechanical variables and driving performance during the golf swing. Journal of sports sciences 28(11): 1251-1259.

86. Cochran, A. and J. Stobbs (1968). The Search For The Perfect Swing. Chicago, Triumph Books.

87. Coleman, S. and D. Anderson (2007). An examination of the planar nature of golf club motion in the swings of experienced players. Journal of sports sciences 25(7): 739-748.

88. Coleman, S. G. S. and A. J. Rankin (2005). A three-dimensional examination of the planar nature of the golf swing. Journal of sports sciences 23(3): 227-234.

89. Cross, R. (2005). A double pendulum swing experiment: In search of a better bat. American Journal of Physics 73: 330.

90. Cross, R. (2009). Mechanics of swinging a bat. American Journal of Physics 77: 36.

91. Cross, R. (2011). A double pendulum model of tennis strokes. American Journal of Physics 79: 470.

92. Healy, A., K. A. Moran, et al. (2011). Analysis of the 5 iron golf swing when hitting for maximum distance. Journal of sports sciences 29(10): 1079-1088.

93. Hellstrom, J. (2009). Competitive elite golf: a review of the relationships between playing results, technique and physique. Sports Medicine 39(9): 723-741.

94. Horan, S. A., K. Evans, et al. (2011). Movement variability in the golf swing of male and female skilled golfers. Medicine & Science in

Sports & Exercise 43(8): 1474.

95. Hume, P. A., J. Keogh, et al. (2005). The role of biomechanics in maximising distance and accuracy of golf shots. Sports Medicine 35(5): 429-449.

96. Jorgensen Jr, T. (1970). On the dynamics of the swing of a golf club. American Journal of Physics 38: 644.

97. Jorgensen, T. P. (1994). The Physics of Golf. New York, Springer.

98. Jorgensen, T. P. and R. K. Adair (1994). The Physics of Golf. Physics Today 47: 71.

99. Kao, J. T., M. Pink, et al. (1995). Electromyographic analysis of the scapular muscles during a golf swing. The American journal of sports medicine 23(1): 19-23.

100. Kelley, H. (1982). The golfing machine, Star System Press, Seattle.

101. Keogh, J. W. L., M. C. Marnewick, et al. (2009). Are anthropometric, flexibility, muscular strength, and endurance variables related to clubhead velocity in low-and high-handicap golfers? The Journal of Strength & Conditioning Research 23(6): 1841.

102. Kim, T. H., R. J. Jagacinski, et al. (2011). Age-related differences in the rhythmic structure of the golf swing. J Mot Behav 43(6): 433-444.

103. Kwon, Y. H. (2009). Kinematic analysis of sports movements: Golf swing plane analysis. 27th International Conference on Biomechanics in Sports. 1.

104. Libkuman, T. M., H. Otani, et al. (2002). Training in timing improves accuracy in golf. The Journal of general psychology 129(1): 77-96.

105. MacKenzie, S. J. (2011). How does shaft flexibility affect the delivery of the clubhead to the ball?.

106. McHardy, A. and H. Pollard (2005). Muscle activity during the golf swing. British journal of sports medicine 39(11): 799-804.

107. Meister, D. W., A. L. Ladd, et al. (2011). Rotational biomechanics of the elite golf swing: benchmarks for amateurs. Journal of applied biomechanics 27(3): 242.

108. Milburn, P. (1982). Summation of segmental velocities in the golf

swing. Medicine and science in sports and exercise 14(1): 60.

109. Neal, R., R. Lumsden, et al. (2008). Segment Interactions: Sequencing and timing in the downswing. Science And Golf V: Proceedings of the World Scientific Congress of Golf D. Crews and R. Lutz. Tempe, Arizona, Ironwood Lithographers: 21-29.

110. Nesbit, S. M. (2005). A three dimensional kinematic and kinetic study of the golf swing. Journal of Sports Science and Medicine 4(4): 499-519.

111. Nesbit, S. M. (2011). Biomechanical study of the golf swing using a full body computer model. Journal of applied golf research.

112. Nesbit, S. M. and R. McGinnis (2009). Kinematic analyses of the golf swing hub path and its role in golfer/club kinetic transfers. Journal of Sports Science and Medicine 8(2): 235-246.

113. Nesbit, S. M. and M. Serrano (2005). Work and power analysis of the golf swing. Journal of Sports Science and Medicine 4(4): 520-533.

114. Parks, D. (2011). Revisiting a classic: the search for the perfect swing. Journal of applied golf research.

115. Parks, D. (2011). Revisiting the search for the perfect swing: muscle activity patterns. Journal of applied golf research.

116. Penner, A. R. (2003). The physics of golf. Reports on Progress in Physics 66: 131.

117. Pickering, W. and G. Vickers (1999). On the double pendulum model of the golf swing. Sports Engineering 2(3): 161-172.

118. Putnam, C. A. (1991). A segment interaction analysis of proximal-to-distal sequential segment motion patterns. Medicine and science in sports and exercise 23(1): 130.

119. Putnam, C. A. (1993). Sequential motions of body segments in striking and throwing skills: descriptions and explanations. Journal of biomechanics 26: 125-135.

120. Sprigings, E. and S. Mackenzie (2002). Examining the delayed release in the golf swing using computer simulation. Sports Engineering 5(1): 23-32.

121. Suzuki, S., S. Haake, et al. (2005). Skill analysis of the wrist release in

golf swing to utilize shaft elasticity. Asia-Pacific congress on sports technology, Australasian sports technology alliance.

122. Tinmark, F., J. Hellström, et al. (2010). Elite golfers' kinematic sequence in full-swing and partial-swing shots. Sports Biomechanics 9(4): 236-244.

123. Torres-Ronda, L., L. Sánchez-Medina, et al. (2011). Muscle strength and golf performance: a critical review. Journal of Sports Science and Medicine 10: 9-18.

124. Vena, A., D. Budney, et al. (2011). Three-dimensional kinematic analysis of the golf swing using instantaneous screw axis theory, part 1: methodology and verification. Sports Engineering 13(3): 105-123.

125. Vena, A., D. Budney, et al. (2011). Three-dimensional kinematic analysis of the golf swing using instantaneous screw axis theory, Part 2: golf swing kinematic sequence. Sports Engineering 13(3): 125-133.

126. Watkins, R. G., G. S. Uppal, et al. (1996). Dynamic electromyographic analysis of trunk musculature in professional golfers. The American journal of sports medicine 24(4): 535-538.

127. Williams Jr, A. (1972). An obscure influence in the golf shot. Journal of Dynamic Systems, Measurement, and Control 94: 289.

## *Talent and practice*

128. Baker, J. (2001). Genes and training for athletic performance revisited. Sportscience 5(2).

129. Baker, J., S. Horton, et al. (2003). Nurturing sport expertise: factors influencing the development of elite athlete. Journal of Sports Science and Medicine 2(1): 1-9.

130. Baron, R. A. and R. A. Henry (2010). How entrepreneurs acquire the capacity to excel: insights from research on expert performance. Strategic Entrepreneurship Journal 4(1): 49-65.

131. Beilock, S. L. and T. H. Carr (2004). From novice to expert performance, Psychology Press.

132. Beilock, S. L., T. H. Carr, et al. (2002). When paying attention becomes counterproductive: Impact of divided versus skill-focused attention on novice and experienced performance of sensorimotor skills. Journal of Experimental Psychology: Applied; Journal of Experimental Psychology: Applied 8(1): 6.

133. Beilock, S. L. and I. M. Lyons (2009). Expertise and the mental simulation of action. Handbook of Imagination and Mental Simulation. K. Markman, B. Klein & J. Suhr, Psychology Press: 21-34.

134. Davids, K. (2001). Genes, Training, and other Constraints on Individual Performance: A Role for Dynamical Systems Theory? Sportsc/eлce 5(2).

135. Ericsson, K. (2000). Expert performance and deliberate practice: An updated excerpt from Ericsson (2000). July 22: 2007.

136. Ericsson, K. A. (2006). The influence of experience and deliberate practice on the development of superior expert performance. The Cambridge handbook of expertise and expert performance. K. A. Ericsson, N. Charness, P. Feltovich and R. R. Hoffman. Cambridge, Cambridge University Press: 685-706.

137. Ericsson, K. A., R. T. Krampe, et al. (1993). The role of deliberate practice in the acquisition of expert performance. Psychological review 100(3): 363.

138. Fox, P. W., S. L. Hershberger, et al. (1996). Genetic and environmental contributions to the acquisition of a motor skill.

139. Gulbin, J. (2006). Why Deliberate Practice isn't Enough.

140. Hopkins, W. (2001). Genes and training for athletic performance. Sportscience 5(1).

141. Milton, J., A. Solodkin, et al. (2007). The mind of expert motor performance is cool and focused. Neuroimage 35(2): 804-813.

142. Missitzi, J., R. Gentner, et al. (2011). Plasticity in human motor cortex is in part genetically determined. The Journal of Physiology 589(2): 297-306.

# Notes

1 Bernard Darwin, Tee Shots and Others; London: Kegan Paul, Trench, Trubner & Co. Ltd. 1911.

2 Peter Lightbown, Annual Review of Golf Coaching, 2010.

3 Bernard Darwin, Tee Shots and Others; London: Kegan Paul, Trench, Trubner & Co. Ltd. 1911.

4 Implicit learning is the learning of complex information or movements, without knowing what has been learnt. It requires minimal – or no – attention.

5 Dynamic systems theory is an alternative to trying to solve complex problems mathematically. It investigates a system's complex dynamics. For applications to the golf swing, see references 68–77. Major contributors are Keith Davids and Paul Glazier.

6 From reference 2.

7 For a discussion of paralysis by analysis, see reference 10.

8 A phrase originally coined by Richard Masters and John Burns, in their book Mind Swings: the Thinking Way to Better Golf.

9 From reference 141.

10 Bernard Darwin, Tee Shots and Others; London: Kegan Paul, Trench, Trubner & Co. Ltd. 1911.

11 William James, Principles of Psychology, 1890.

12 See reference 53 for a review of external focus in golf.

13 Comments paraphrased from a TV programme. For a full review of choking, see references 59 and 60 by Sian Beilock.

14 The pink elephant example started life as a white bear. Social psychologist Daniel Wegner and colleagues studied thought suppression by instructing participants to avoid all thoughts of a white bear. The pink elephant is often used in relation to sport.

15 A video recording of James Bruen's swing can be seen at http://www.youtube.com/watch?v=9_qRG1HRh4o (accessible as of August 2012).

16 Blacksmiths' hammer swings were studied by N.A. Bernstein and results reported in the book: The Coordination and Regulation of Movements. Oxford; UK. Pergamon. 1967.

17 Expert shooters were studied by G.A. Arutyunyan and colleagues and results reported in the book: Investigation of Aiming at a Target, 1968.

18 The concept of a 'perfect golf swing' was first proposed by Cochran and Stobbs (reference 86). For follow-up articles, see references 114 and 115 by Dan Parks.

19 Adaptability and the ability to self-correct are features of the golf swing supported by dynamic systems theory.

20 Swing-to-swing variation is a manifestation of movement variability. See references 71 and 75, by Paul Glazier.

21 The technical name for limitations is *constraints*. Follow-up information can be found in references 69 and 76, by Keith Davids and Simon Jenkins, respectively.

22 Attributed to Geoffrey Boycott, Yorkshire and England cricketer.

23 A term first used by Kelso J.A.S. and Ding M. 'Fluctuations, intermittency and controllable chaos in biological coordination'. In: Newell, K.M. and Corcos D, editors, Variability and Motor Control. Champaign, Il.; Human Kinetics. 1993. 291-316.

24 Title of Edward Lorenz's lecture given to the American Association for the Advancement of Science, 1979.

25 Taken from an interview with Fredrik Tuxen – inventor of Trackman™ radar-based swing/ball tracking system, reported in the Journal of Applied Golf Research, March 2011.

26 The technical name for a muscular chain is *kinetic chain*, or *biokinetic chain*.

27 See reference 127

28 The motion of a double pendulum – although straightforward during the golf swing phase, is chaotic thereafter.

29 An interactive model of a double pendulum can be found at http://www.myphysicslab.com/dbl_pendulum.html (accessible as of August 2012).

30 A passive release is also referred to as a *natural* release. At a point in the downswing – the point of natural release – the wrists passively start to unhinge.

31 Bernard Darwin, Tee Shots and Others; London: Kegan Paul, Trench, Trubner & Co. Ltd. 1911.

32 See references 135–137 by Anders Ericsson for a review.

33 A phrase coined by Anders Ericsson – see reference 136.

34 A phrase first used by Bernstein N.A. The Coordination and Regulation of Movement. Oxford; UK. Pergamon. 1967.

35 See reference 136 by Anders Ericsson for a review.

36 The percentage of fast twitch muscle fibres determine the speed at which a muscle can contract. They are required in speed and power sports. Slow twitch muscle fibres contract slowly and are required for endurance sports.

37 See references 134 and 140 by Keith Davids and Will Hopkins, for contributions to this debate.

38 A phrased first used by Lewontin R. The Triple Helix: Gene, Organism and Environment. Cambridge, MA; Harvard University press.

39 A discussion of skill-related warm-up can be found in reference 4, by Robert Ajemian and colleagues.

40 A phrase coined by Beilock and Carr – reference 59.

41 Bernard Darwin, Tee Shots and Others; London: Kegan Paul, Trench, Trubner & Co. Ltd. 1911.

42 Some explanations use the related concept of centrifugal force. This approach is equally valid and in some ways easier to understand. The centrifugal force is equal to the centripetal force and acts in the opposite direction.

# Index

Made in the USA
Lexington, KY
18 July 2013